DON'T LET

MeCry

MY STORY OF MY BATTLE
WITH BREAST CANCER

DON'T LET *MeCry*

MY STORY OF MY BATTLE WITH BREAST CANCER

MEMOIRS

Cirencester

Published by Memoirs

MEMOIRS
PUBLISHING

25 Market Place, Cirencester, Gloucestershire, GL7 2NX
info@memoirsbooks.co.uk www.memoirspublishing.com

ISBN 978-1-909544-37-6

Breast Cancer Care is here for anyone affected by
breast cancer. We bring people together, provide information and
support, and campaign for improved standards of care.
We use our understanding of people's experience of breast cancer
and our clinical expertise in everything we do.

**Visit www.breastcancercare.org.uk or call our free
helpline on 0808 800 6000.**

Registered charity in England and Wales 1017658

Registered charity in Scotland SC038104

INTRODUCTION

Today is the 13th December 2010. It is 9.30 pm and I'm thinking about Christmas. This time last year, it was just another day, a day I wanted to finish as quickly as it had started. A year ago, three weeks before Christmas 2009, my mum lost her fight with MS after spending seven weeks in hospital.

Three months later I was diagnosed with breast cancer. And that is what my story is about.

So I'm thinking that today is a new day, other days will continue past today and my life and the story that goes with it will go on. If I can share these words with just one other person, someone who needs to know, someone who through reading them will help them understand what they will face over the coming months, or find the answers they desperately need, then it'll all be worth it.

So this is my story, the story of what can only be described as a pretty crap twelve months in my life. This is the story of my battle with breast cancer.

PROLOGUE

Have you ever woken up and thought, 'This is going to be a bad day'?

Have you ever cried so much you can't breathe?

Have you ever been so angry it hurts?

No one would ever have known that I spent hours trawling the internet to find miracle cures. Lorenzo's oil, maybe that would help, stem cell treatment, anything, there must be a cure, or at least hope…

Some illnesses are so twisted.

Some illnesses squeeze the life out of you, not just the living breathing, but also the walking talking.

Some illnesses take your dignity.

If you spent fifteen years knowing you had MS, would you still be smiling? Would you still be fighting? When you've seen pure courage, when you've seen laughter, how can you show weakness in the face of fear?

I heard a saying recently 'What doesn't kill you makes you stronger'. I'm still testing that theory. My Mum proved it, by the fight and spirit she displayed throughout those fifteen years battling an illness, the same illness I never did find a 'miracle' cure for, so this book is written in dedication to her.

I will get through the next year with her strength, her courage and her drive for life.

Thursday 3rd December 2009

The journey to the hospital seemed to take forever. When we arrived I hesitated to go in. I didn't want to accept the inevitable.

If someone had said to me seven weeks before that my mum would go into hospital, end up in critical care and slowly go downhill until there was no hope, I would have thought they were mad. Then again, if someone had told me that this time next year I'd be bald - well, you get the point. We all think we're indestructible, but we're not.

It was 9.30 pm and I was now alone, just my mum and me. The radio was playing by the bed. I don't remember why, but of all the music I heard that night Don't Speak by No Doubt is the only one I can remember.

Friday 4th December 2009 – 1:20am

There are few words to describe how it felt, how it still feels. Emotions are very personal and hard to share. Numbness, emptiness, overwhelming sadness, guilt, anger, and the list can go on forever.

Goodnight Mum - Thank you for giving me the strength to face the next twelve months.

CHAPTER ONE

Why me? Well, why not? That's what I think if my mind ever starts going down that path. I force myself to think that's there's nothing I can do about it, no magic to take it all away. So I keep going, taking each day as it comes. That's what you have to do and keep on doing, until time passes and this all becomes a distant memory.

Some time in February 2010 I became aware of a lump. It's strange, as I don't actually remember when or how I found it; I just instinctively started feeling it, every morning and every night. It was a solid lump. My skin didn't move over it and I knew, I just knew, it wasn't right. It was alien to my body, and I was scared.

Fear can stop you from doing anything, but at some point you can't go on ignoring it. What if? I was busy, too busy to go to the doctor's, but at some point I knew I had to get it confirmed. I knew I couldn't keep ignoring it.

It took me about two weeks to pluck up the courage. I had only ever known two people to have breast cancer and neither had survived. In honesty, if I had asked more questions back then, I would have understood why, but I didn't, so here I was, staring fear directly in the face. If it was confirmed, would that be it, game over?

I reluctantly booked an appointment, and when I arrived I explained my symptoms to the doctor. She asked me to get undressed so she could feel the lump. I knew from that point that this wasn't going to be simple.

She clearly wasn't happy with what she could feel and told me she was going to refer me for some tests. I remember asking her questions like 'Is a lump more worrying if it's solid and doesn't move, or if you can move it under your skin?' The answer didn't much matter, not just because I didn't really listen, but because I knew this lump was bad news. I've been living in my own skin for long enough to know when something's not right.

It's weird, because we've all had something that we think could be bad, but know in your heart it will come to nothing. This was different. I was trying so hard to make myself believe it would be nothing and I knew other people would think the same, but I knew, I knew this was bad.

After the doctor's appointment, I was meeting a friend, Teresa, for lunch. When I arrived at her house, one of the first things she said to me was ' How are you?' Well I couldn't lie, I would need to master that art for a later date, for everyone else.

Sunday 14th March

I had received a letter from the hospital a few days before and my appointment was in the morning, but I had kept quiet. I had no one to go with and the realisation of what I might be facing was starting to scare me. I didn't really want to go alone, but I also didn't want to worry anyone.

After a battle with myself over what to do, I decided to show the letter to my housemate, Kate. She had seen the envelope downstairs and wondered what it was for. We sat in my bedroom and I told her what had been going on over the last couple of weeks. However I was adamant at this point that I didn't want anyone else to know.

Monday 15th March

Suddenly breast cancer is everywhere, on posters, TV, in the news and on the radio. It's one of those things - as time goes on I see it more and more. Did I just never notice it before, or was I not looking? Either way my eyes have now well and truly been opened to this illness.

Kate dropped me off at the hospital in the morning, something she would get used to doing over the next few months. I didn't really know what to expect and sat there nervously until I was called through.

My first port of call was the breast specialist. She felt the lump and initially lifted my spirits as she said it didn't feel abnormal, but she wanted to send me for a mammogram so she could be sure.

So I waited. I wondered what was going through everyone's minds. Were they thinking the same as me? There were a lot of women in the waiting room and they kept coming and going.

We were all in our own worlds, all dealing with whatever the day was throwing at us. There was a lady there who seemed to know me. I knew her too, but neither of us could place where from or how. We didn't say much. We just waited.

I didn't have to wait for too long.

The first part is to put the attractive hospital gown on. Am I really the only person who can never work out how to do these damn things up - should I tie it at the back, or at the front? I decided on the front, but I'm still not sure!

I had seen a TV programme where a mammogram was described as not dissimilar to a robot manhandling you – they weren't joking! You place your breast on a plate and another comes on top to squash it. I believe the correct way of explaining this would be to say your breasts are compressed. The flatter your breast, the better the picture. So it's squashed, or compressed to within an inch of its life, which means to a just-bearable level. At this point a picture is taken, then you are released and the process goes on again, using all possible angles.

I could have been thinking anything at this stage, but my brain decided to wonder what would happen if there was a power cut and I was stuck with my breast between two plates, in pain. I didn't consider the manual release until I had stopped panicking! 'Please hurry up and get this over with' was all I could think.

Back in the waiting room in a gown, and now the fire alarm started going off. Bugger, it's March, it's cold and I'm in a hospital gown, is this really happening?

After what turned out to be a false alarm, I got called back in for another mammogram. I wasn't expecting that. I guess they needed better pictures. Here we go again with the robot!

Now I noticed that the waiting room was slowly emptying and I was told I needed an ultrasound examination. Ultrasound is used when abnormalities are found with a mammogram. The procedure is quite simple. They put some gel on a thing called a transducer. You lie on your back with your arm raised above your head and glide the transducer over the area they are examining. This shows images on a screen. There's no pain, just a slight arm ache, depending on how long the procedure takes.

I lay on the bed watching the screen, pretending I knew what I was looking at. The doctor didn't say a word, which I found a little unnerving. She was measuring things on the screen and it wasn't looking good.

When it was over I went back to my seat in the waiting room. I really was the only person left there now. I felt sad. I wanted the day to end.

After a short wait, my name was called and I went back in to see the consultant, who gently explained that it looked concerning and they wanted to perform a biopsy - today. I felt overwhelmed. I started to realise that this was the start of a new chapter in my life, one that was either going to break me or make me stronger.

Initially, I cracked. I was taken to see a breast care specialist, who gently talked to me about the possibility of cancer and how they would help. Lovely as these people are, why is it that as soon as you talk to them, you just start crying? I don't do counselling well and probably never will. I didn't speak much, I just listened. I never have been much of a speaker and that's not about to change.

I really can't tell you what she said, as clearly nothing went in. Afterwards I was desperate to get out, so I left the hospital and went and sat on a wall outside. I didn't know what to do, or what to think, so I called Kate. Only two people were aware I was there, and she was one of them. I was terrified and I didn't want to go back in.

Kate came to the hospital and I got back into my gown and we waited. What she didn't tell me then was that she had spotted a lady, a larger lady, in a gown, who had an obvious shape representing a mastectomy with no reconstruction. She only told me this later. It was probably a wise move.

I was called in for the biopsy, and this was the part I was dreading. I knew nothing about biopsies, but the word didn't sound like something I was likely to enjoy.

As I lay on the bed a small comedy developed. First the bed got stuck - they couldn't get it to move up or down - and then the ultrasound refused to work. Once that drama was over, it was time for my first needle. I have a mild phobia about needles, probably along with 95% of the population.

When I was a child, the dentists always used gas to knock me out, as they always had problems with injections. My first memory of my needle phobia was during a visit to remove a tooth. I was too old for gas, so today they would attempt to put me to sleep with an injection. After about six attempts, I finally drifted off, a little traumatised.

I had the weirdest experience; I woke up - not physically, just the part of my brain that controls my hearing and thoughts. I couldn't feel anything, I couldn't move and I couldn't talk, but I remember hearing the roots as they pulled the tooth out, and fear gripped me. Then it was over and my senses started to return. I remember waking up and looking towards my feet. It felt as if I was on a slide and was going to slide off the bed and through the door.

Was any of that real? I have no idea, but it set the stage for a very real phobia.

The doctor explained that I would be injected with local anaesthetic, to numb the area where the biopsies would be performed. I was shown the piece of equipment that would be used and she said I would hear a click, which she demonstrated. This would be the actual biopsy and she would warn me first.

I have never wanted something to end so much. I don't believe it was supposed to be painful, but of my six biopsies, I felt three. Maybe the local anaesthetic wasn't strong enough. It felt a bit like being shot with something and the inside of your breast being hit really hard.

I swear that every time I have something needle-related, it goes wrong. I was beginning to think that the worst part of this was going to be my fear of needles - and convincing the doctors I wasn't just soft.

Teresa came with me to get the results. I can only describe the hospital waiting room as like a cattle market. It was packed and there was barely a place to sit. It became very evident that there was an overload of patients and few consultants on this day. The nurses at the reception desks were getting stressed, as people were complaining about the wait. I can't remember how long we waited, but my stomach was in knots by the time I was called.

I knew I didn't want to see the male consultant, as I had worked out that he was the one giving out bad news. So when I was called through, my heart sank when he smiled at me.

Mr Cummins, who was to become my consultant and surgeon, explained that I had first-stage grade one breast cancer. Cancers are graded one to three, with grade one indicating a slower-growing one. The stages are the extent of the spread of cancer and its size. They had caught it early and the prognosis was good. He didn't at this stage believe it would have spread.

Then he hit me with the news that was to completely numb me, something I hadn't even considered and never really accepted right up to the day of surgery - I still haven't. I was going to have to have a mastectomy. He told me that they had detected more then one lump. This meant that they couldn't just cut it out by performing a lumpectomy, as having more than one lump shows that it may come back again.

I don't think I really acknowledged those words and it's so hard to explain the feeling, as if I was about to have something taken away from me, that I wouldn't be whole and it didn't feel right. I had no knowledge of this procedure and really did believe that they just cut your breast off, then reconstructed it using skin from other parts of your body. Just the thought of it was doing my head in!

However, I couldn't have been more wrong. He went on to explain the procedure, though to be honest, I was in so much shock that I wasn't listening, so it would be a little later before I would come to fully understand what would actually happen.

When we arrived home, I called Kate. My mind had gone into overdrive, and all I wanted at that point was my BUPA details from work (I work for a cinema chain). I was very fortunate to have BUPA cover and I recognise that fact. I called them to start off what was to be a long process.

I still wasn't ready to tell anyone yet, although I knew Kate had told my boss. We all work together and he was with her when she left to come to the hospital on Monday. He is also a friend, so I called him to confirm the news. From this point onwards, I couldn't have been more supported by my employers. Little things like that can make a big difference and I will always be thankful to them for making my life easy in this area.

However, in shock I may have been, but I still decided to go into work that night. I wanted to tell my team what was happening, as I was well aware that this would affect them too.

It was one of those random days when my whole management team were in. So I called them all to the office and told them very calmly that I had been diagnosed that morning with breast cancer.

CHAPTER TWO

Thursday 18th March

I now became obsessed with chemotherapy. It took up all my thoughts - would I need it or wouldn't I? I didn't want it, I knew that much. I couldn't go through with it, not now. Only a few friends and the people at work knew about this. How would I hide chemotherapy?

I had my first consultation with Mr Cummins at Parkside Hospital in Wimbledon. My friends were being great. It was obvious I wasn't going to go through this alone, yet I still couldn't tell people outside this group and I still couldn't tell my family.

My friend Tessa drove me in and not knowing where it was, we gave ourselves 45 minutes to get there. In fact it only took 20. This hospital is one I was to become well acquainted with over the coming months, and so would Tessa and Kate.

I'd had twenty-four hours for the news to sink in and was starting to feel a sense of acceptance. Everything was happening so quickly. This was the first time I started thinking that there was nothing I could do about it, so I would just have to deal with it. I was trying to be tough, but deep down all I really wanted to do was curl up in a ball and make it all go away.

At the hospital Mr Cummins explained at length what type of cancer I had and assured me that the prognosis was good, so it was all about how we were going to deal with it to give me the best results. He told me about the plastic surgeon he wanted me to meet, who would perform the surgery with him. Before that though I would need some investigative surgery, which would be arranged for the following week at Kingston hospital.

Tuesday 23rd March

They needed to know if the cancer had spread to my lymph nodes, so I had an appointment booked for an operation to remove them for testing. I was having what was called a sentinel lymph node biopsy. In short the sentinel lymph node is the first one - if the cancer has reached it, it might have spread.

They started with what is called lymph node mapping, so I was going to Kingston Hospital in preparation for the operation tomorrow. I was to visit the nuclear medicine department, where they would inject a radioactive liquid into me. My understanding was that the surgeon would then inject a blue dye, which would stain the lymph node tissue so it could be easily identified.

When I arrived at the hospital I was to go first to the private ward I would be staying in the next day to have swabs done to check for MRSA. As expected, nothing went to plan. I clearly hadn't listened properly, as I had no idea where to go for the swab tests and it was starting to look as if I would be late. No one seemed to be able to help me, as they didn't understand what I was looking for, so I went straight to nuclear medicine. Thankfully, although I was now late for their appointment, they did help and after a few phone calls they found where I should have been and off I headed.

When I arrived back, I went into a small waiting room. A man was in there with his daughter and I could see the door where the testing takes place was slightly ajar. A baby started screaming and I heard a lady's voice trying to soothe it. This sent shivers through me - if a baby screamed that much, what were they doing to it? The little girl went up to the door, but her Dad called her away. They must have been family, and she was as worried as I was about what was happening in that room.

It was now my turn. I lay on the bed and was told they would be injecting some radioactive liquid into me, which might hurt a bit. They weren't joking, I'm not going to lie, it bloody hurt! The injection was in my areola, and as they released the liquid an indescribable pain swept through the area. That was and still is one of the few times I have let out a scream in pain. I wanted it to stop and was close to begging for it to do so.

I wondered what else I would have to go through before this was all over. It was the not knowing, all the little things you had to have done leading up to surgery, all the investigations, all the injections. How many hospital visits would I need?

When I arrived home, I rang a friend of mine. It was her

daughter's sixth birthday the next day and I needed to be able to get out of calling her, as they didn't know. You see her mum had lost her battle to breast cancer 11 years ago. I couldn't tell her - I wasn't ready. So instead I did the birthday wishes a day early and made my excuses.

Wednesday 24th March

Today was the big day, my first operation, my first time in theatre (if you ignore me being knocked out for the removal of my wisdom teeth) and I was pretty nervous. I still had issues with believing I might wake up during the operation, even though it was pretty clear that that was not going to happen. I wasn't really thinking about the outcome at this point, as I couldn't entertain the idea that it might have spread. I just ignored the fact that this might be a reality and made myself believe I'd be OK.

Once in my room in the hospital ward, I had to confirm details and sign forms. They needed a next of kin, but I couldn't give them the details of any of my family as they still didn't know and I wasn't about to tell them. I had this idea that I could get through this whole scenario without them knowing. I didn't want to burden them, I didn't want them worrying and I didn't want them going through the whole hospital thing again. Also, stupid as it may sound, I felt very much as if this was a bit of a girl's disease and not something I felt comfortable talking about, so my girlfriends were all I really needed. Even then I felt I didn't have the energy to keep going over it with different people, so the fewer who knew, the better. So on this occasion, I ended up giving Kate's details. I know - kind of selfish, what if something had gone wrong?

It feels as if you keep answering the same questions over and over, but I knew it had to be done. I guess there's always a risk of doing the wrong operation on the wrong person. So I put on a hospital gown and waited for the porter. When he arrived, he insisted that I lie on the trolley to be taken to surgery, despite the fact I was perfectly capable of walking. Oh well, I guess in the 21st century health and safety rules.

I had never been in theatre, so I didn't know what to expect. I was wheeled into a room and the doctors immediately began to hook me up to things. Here comes the needle...

I didn't even know they were about to put me to sleep, but next thing I knew I was waking up in the recovery room. I suddenly felt overwhelmed and the need to get out of hospital was at the forefront of my mind. I was up and dressed as quickly as I could, and out of the door asking to go home. I thought I was fine, so I just walked through the hospital and out to Kate's waiting car. However, the second the air hit me, I felt dizzy and the car journey home was horrid. I felt nauseous all the way.

The radioactive dye had turned my wee green. Luckily I had been warned of this, or it would have given me quite a shock. That evening, I just lay on the sofa feeling sorry for myself. Thankfully the sickly feeling soon passed.

I didn't have to wait long for the results, as today I had a consultation booked with Mr Cummins. Initially my spirits were lifted again as he told me I didn't have two lumps after all; the second was a lymph node, not a tumour. I believe lymph nodes are in your armpit, yet this one was in my breast. Apparently lots of women are like this, so I wasn't abnormal.

I thought that surely I could have a lumpectomy now? The answer was simple - no. Unfortunately for me, this lymph node was showing that the cancer had spread to it, so although it was confined to my breast so far, with evidence of it spreading it could return if I just had the lumps cut out. The mastectomy was still the only option. I felt sick. Something inside of me could be killing me, but I had no control. No medicine, no healthy diet, no exercise was going to get me out of this one. I can only imagine the pain of the woman who is told her cancer has spread. So I had to get over it. I had to cope with the mastectomy and whatever else was going to be thrown at me, and thank my lucky stars that it was caught early.

It was at this point that we had our first real conversation about chemotherapy. Despite what I said earlier, I really had a bee in my bonnet about this. It was the one thing I would fight off for a long time, as I was so frightened about having it. Then there was the stupid belief that I had about not telling my family. I wasn't thinking straight and honestly believed I could get through this without anyone knowing.

Because I was at stage one, I was told I wouldn't need chemo to shrink the tumour; it was more of a precaution to stop it returning. I had a choice. I could have it first, then have the surgery, or I could have it afterwards. However, it didn't matter how many choices I had, I was in pieces. I tried the best I could to explain why I didn't want chemo, what I had been through over the last few months and why that meant I didn't want my family knowing. My surgeon was great. He seemed to understand that I needed time and suggested we should organise the operation first and then let me see an oncologist to advise me whether chemo was really necessary or not. I guess he knew at that point that I would be told it was, but I got the feeling he didn't want to upset me any more.

So the next stage was now about understanding what the operation would consist of and when and where it would happen.

I don't think any of this had really sunk in yet. My emotions were up and down and it was almost as if this was all happening around me, not to me. I think when you are faced with a shit time, you almost switch off to it and just let it pass, taking each day at a time. I couldn't think about tomorrow, as it scared me too much.

Wednesday 7th April

Mr Cummins referred me to a brilliant plastic surgeon called Paul Harris, who would take me through the next stages. So I now had an appointment at the Cromwell Hospital in London to meet him. The reception resembled a plush hotel, which for me was good, as I didn't feel I was in a hospital. However I also felt a bit out of place and was unsure what I was supposed to be doing. It soon became clear that it was all about filling in more forms, then waiting.

I spent a while trying to guess which one Mr Harris was, as you do, to try and pass time. The nerves were starting to get the better of me. Then finally, I was called through.

Mr Harris was kind and patient. At first he sat and spoke gently to me, putting me at ease. Then I had to get undressed so he could see my shape and get an idea what surgery was best. In other words I had to get half naked and have a strange man stare at my breasts! For those who think that may be uncomfortable, it was actually the easiest part - part of the package, I guess. We then sat down and he explained the options available to me. He clearly wanted the best cosmetic results for me, not just for now but for my future. This was where I began to understand what was really involved with a mastectomy.

I was to have a procedure they call skin sparing, and possibly nipple sparing. What this means is that your nipple and essentially all your breast tissue is removed, leaving the outside skin untouched. The breast is then filled with tissue from the abdomen or buttocks. So in theory, other then slight scarring around the nipple, it would look the same as it did before. This made me feel a whole lot better.

He went on to explain the three options that were open to me. (I think I've got this right):

Option one – Have implants. Simple but not cosmetically sound. He wasn't advising me to have this one and I wasn't interested anyway.

Option two – Using a flap from your back (a latissimus dorsi flap). This is a muscle in your back which the surgeon uses, along with the skin and fat covering it, to make the new breast. He didn't seem keen on this idea and I switched off when he mentioned the word 'muscle' as I didn't like the idea of any of my muscles being cut. It might also have needed implants, and I wasn't keen on anything unatural.

Option three – DIEP flap. This is where you have your stomach cut, hip to hip, but on the bikini line. Skin and fatty tissue in the abdomen are then used for the reconstruction of the breast. A different version of this is called the TRAM flap, but with that procedure, muscle is also cut.

The DIEP procedure is the trickiest of the three and the surgeon also has to remove and reconnect blood vessels. However, regardless of how complicated it is, you end up with what can only be described as something similar to a tummy tuck and a boob job.

This was the option he felt would be best for me. It is however a major operation, one which would take six to eight hours and require a long recovery. It was overwhelming, especially since I had told all my workmates, I'd only be off for a few weeks!

Mr Harris showed me photos of operations he had performed in the past, I guess this was to help put my mind at rest, but in all honesty I don't think I was really taking much of it in. It was going to take a little while longer before the scope of it all hit me.

He explained that I would need to have a CT scan first as he needed to know where my muscles were. This would take place at the Royal Marsden in Chelsea, which was also where my operation was to take place. He also arranged for me to go back and see him again, as he appreciated that it was a lot to take in and would give me time for any questions.

April

Everything was arranged very quickly. By now I had told a few friends, but still not my family. On the day of the scan, I arranged to meet one friend, Jayne, afterwards in London.

I remember being nervous about what they did, as I had no idea what a CT scan involved. When I arrived I was told I would have some dye injected first (again!) and my understanding at the time was that it would help show up the blood vessels. Of course that may be a slightly incorrect account, as sometimes when people tell me things, I only hear what I want to hear, either that or I don't really understand!

As I sat in the waiting room I kept seeing people being called through, then returning with what I can only describe as a big bandage covering something on their arm. When you've never really spent time in hospital, seeing things like that is scary. I had no expectations. I had no idea what happens and I had no idea what the bandages were covering or if I was about to get the same.

My nerves were starting to get the better of me by the time I was called through. The nurse told me she was going to put a cannula (a narrow tube) in me for them to use during the scan to inject the dye. I can't remember what I said, but it was something along the lines of being scared of needles again, to which I have a vague memory of her suggesting I should think of something nice, like a beach!

Back out in the waiting room with my bandage, I sat and wondered what was coming next. Thankfully I didn't have to wait for very long, as I was soon called back through.

The machine that does the CT scan is like a box with a hole in it. It is positioned over a bed which you lie on. It's like a tunnel round the bed, except that it moves over you rather than containing you.

Even though I knew it wasn't going to hurt me, I was still nervous. I was worried about the injection, as I didn't really understand what they meant by injecting into the cannula. Would I feel it?

The doctor told me to listen to the machine's instructions and follow them; A little face would light up on the box to prompt me. It was important that I didn't move. It always worries me when people say that, as you're guaranteed to get an itch or something. They then left the room while the scan took place. I guess that's because of the radioactive emissions. The tunnel then started to move over me. When it got to a certain point, I was told to hold my breath for a few seconds, then breathe out. This happened a couple of times. Then the doctor returned to the room and injected the dyed liquid into the cannula, which I didn't feel. He told me it might cause a number of sensations, such as a hot flush or a metallic taste in the mouth; some people feel as if they have wet themselves. Luckily I only experienced the first two. The hot flush was weird. It would have been scary if I hadn't been warned. The whole of my body went hot, inside and out.

When it was over, I was told to sit back in the waiting room and drink lots of water. I was asked to stay for about half an hour, in case I had a bad reaction. I waited for about fifteen minutes, and then unfortunately I had a choking fit, which was really embarrassing. After downing a few glasses of water, though still unable to breathe properly, I left.

I went into London to meet Jayne, who was also having a crap time of it healthwise, so we spent the rest of the day discussing the fact that we were like a couple of old ladies getting ill and miserable!

CHAPTER THREE

I received confirmation of my operation date, which was 29th April. I would be admitted on the 28th - my 37th birthday. This would be one to remember. In fact, if I'm honest, I felt really pissed off. Getting cancer is bad enough, but to be in hospital on my birthday too! I felt really miserable about the whole thing.

When you get to this point you still can't really imagine what it will be like after the operation. As long as you're walking, talking and are physically OK, you can't begin to form any pictures in your mind of not being able to do something, not being able to walk, not being able to stand up straight, not being able to lie down flat and so on. That's why, up to this point, I was convinced that this little inconvenience wouldn't interfere with the holiday I had booked in Amsterdam. I was sure I could have the op and be up and about within a week. So the timing, the exact week I was due to go, didn't really go down too well and just made me more miserable.

It was the Easter holidays and my dad was looking after my nephew for a couple of weeks. I figured it would be the first time since losing Mum that he had something good to focus on, so this was just another excuse for me not to tell him. But the operation was approaching fast and I knew I couldn't go through it without letting my family know.

Finally I plucked up the courage to call my brother. I didn't know what I was going to say or how I was going to say it, but I had to tell him. I can't remember the words that came out, but he must know me too well, because without hesitation he offered to tell Dad when he picked Daniel (my nephew) up. It was a relief, as I wanted him to be told face to face, but I was clearly never going to do it.

The weekend came and as expected I got a call from my dad. His first words were 'I hear you have a little problem'. I guess I had read him wrong. I wasn't sure how he'd react, so I was probably worrying too much. He told me that nothing shocked him any more, and with that I realised he was probably going to take this in his stride, just as I had had to.

We spoke about Mum and what she had been through, the hospitals, the injections, but you can't really compare. She had had an illness that was progressive and with no known cure. I had an illness that with a bit of luck would be successfully treated so I could get on with my life, if with a bit of caution. So it was back to being brave. Who was I to moan when there were people who were going through far worse things than me. Again, I figured that I would just have to take whatever was thrown at me and get on with it.

I still told him not to come to the hospital. Friends were fine, but I didn't want my family there if I was going to look ill. It was best they waited till I got home. I can be very stubborn, but in hindsight, I probably didn't think what they would have wanted, and that was wrong.

Monday 19th April

I was booked to go back to the Royal Marsden to have pre-operation examinations. I was sent a leaflet explaining what this would involve, but I barely read it as I decided it would only worry me if needles were involved.

I arrived at the hospital and was directed to the department I wanted. I think it was the same part of the hospital I would be staying in after the main operation. When I sat down everything started feeling surreal. I was taking in my surroundings and wondering what the next few months would have in store for me.

There was a lady in a headscarf reading a book, and I was trying not to stare, but today I couldn't help it. I knew that this was a very relevant picture for me. I knew I would probably be in that seat somewhere down the line. I started wondering what I would look like if I lost my hair, but no, I couldn't and wouldn't accept that as a real prospect.

A nurse called my name and took me off to do the tests. From memory the ones she did were weight, height and a blood test, which was the first blood test, to my memory, I had ever had. My stomach was in knots. She tied something around my arm and told me to clench my fist. She had found a vein, but as predicted, it didn't work and she had to try again. To be fair, she was good and it didn't hurt too much.

I can't remember too much more of this visit, except having a chat to a male nurse. I guess he had to check I was fit for the operation. One thing I did discover, by luck, was that I shouldn't be taking Anadin prior to my op as it thins your blood and may stop it clotting. I take Anadin on an almost daily basis, so I guess it was lucky I mentioned it.

I also suffered another choking fit in the waiting room and wondered if it was nerve related.

Wednesday 21ˢᵗ April

I had a final appointment with Mr Harris before the operation. Up to now there had been a lot to take in, so this was the opportunity to go back and get answers to all the questions I was bound to have. It was hard though, as I didn't know what to ask. It was more about how long it would take to get better. My friend Claire came with me to give moral support and to ask questions I might not think of. The one thing most people seem to be really interested in is the reconstruction of the nipple. Would it or would it not be permanently erect?

I don't recall him actually giving an answer to that particular question, and I was too embarrassed to carry that conversation on. The lesson here is not to let your friends go to appointments with you, even if you do appreciate the questions!

I needed to know how long it would take for me to get better. I was young, fit and healthy, so he didn't think it would take too long, but he told me I would be looking at at least six to eight weeks before I should consider returning to work. I still believed I would be fine much quicker, as I couldn't comprehend what it would be like, having never had such a major operation. He had mentioned before that one of his patients was up and riding a horse within six weeks, but others were still struggling six months on. I decided there and then that I would be like the horse rider. I mean, surely I would be fine - right?

It was an evening appointment, so I had gone straight from work, as the train journey was easier. I had intended returning afterwards, but something overwhelmed me during this appointment and on the journey back I felt quite low. I certainly couldn't focus on work now, so I went straight home instead. I felt quite guilty, as I'd promised my team I wouldn't let this interfere with work until I had no choice. I guess I was wrong.

All I now seemed to be doing was going backwards and forwards to hospital for tests and consultations. I tried to block most of it out as I wasn't liking hospitals too much now. They reminded me of what my mum had gone through and this had taken over my focus on grieving, which made me angry.

Wednesday 28th April

I spoke to the hospital and they told me I didn't have to stay all day. I just needed to check in and have an injection at some point, but other than that I could go out and celebrate. So I arranged a meal in Chelsea with a few friends later that day. I was so relieved, as I could think of nothing worse then sitting there all day, willing the hours to pass.

Teresa and Kate came with me to check in. When we arrived at the hospital we went straight to the ward detailed on my letter, only to be met by blank faces. Something had gone wrong and I didn't seem to have a room. I was beginning to think that I was one seriously unlucky person!

The nurses told us the bed had been used for an emergency, but someone was due to leave today, so we shouldn't have to wait long. However, we were taken off by a lady who took us to her office to try and get to the bottom of what was going on. I ended up leaving my bags at the hospital and we went out for lunch, leaving them to sort it out.

I remember it being a sunny day and thinking that at least something was going right. We decided to find a pub to have lunch in before returning to the hospital, when I hoped the bed saga would have been sorted out. Later in the day some more friends joined us and we all went out for an evening meal. It felt a bit odd trying to celebrate my birthday, but I was grateful that they were all there and I wasn't alone, although every time I stopped talking I got butterflies in fear of what was to come.

Unfortunately, when we got back to the hospital the room still hadn't been sorted. In fact even a bed hadn't been organised at that point, so they found us an empty room to wait in. Not long after, they took us to one of the main wards. I remember feeling miserable, drained of any emotion. I didn't want to be in a ward, not tonight, not ever.

They had to give me an injection. I think it was a blood thinning one, and it really stung. They then said I could go out again and come back later, so the five of us hit the local pub. My mind wasn't really on celebrating though, I just wanted the night to be over, then tomorrow to be over, then fast forward the rest of the year.

It wasn't too late when I went back to the hospital. I put my pyjamas on and pulled the curtains shut around my bed. I tried to listen to my Ipod, but couldn't concentrate. I just lay there, anticipation of tomorrow's operation playing on my mind. I quietly sobbed to myself and lay awake the entire night, willing the hours to pass.

Thursday 29th April

The day of the operation dawned and it still wasn't real. It was a weird feeling, almost like grief. I couldn't get my head around the fact that I was about to have my breast lopped off, or rather the inside removed, then refilled again all in one go! What would it be like when I woke up? Would I be in pain? Could I really be knocked out for eight hours?

I knew I would never have any feeling in that breast again, or on the part of my stomach they were cutting, and that knowledge wasn't registering. I couldn't imagine having no feeling.

If I were to explain how I was really feeling at this point, I would have to say 'sick to the stomach'. It was almost like a really bad case of butterflies. Then suddenly I would be overcome with it all and the feeling of grief for what I was about to go through was unbearable. I had to try and block it all out, but it was hard. I wanted it to all be over. So there I was standing in the ward with my curtains still drawn around my bed, feeling as if I was on a bad roller coaster ride and couldn't get off. I was just standing there staring, waiting for someone to come, willing the time to pass.

Mr Harris arrived at around 7 am. He gently spoke to me about the operation and tried to put my mind at ease. I just wanted to cry. I didn't want to go through with it, and I was suddenly more scared then I'd ever been in my life, but had no way of stopping it. I knew I had to go through with it, so I just tried to shut my mind down and not think about it, which for the record is not easy when you're standing half naked with someone drawing over you with a big black marker pen! I also had to go through the signing of consent forms, which I barely read.

I then felt the need to have a shower. I figured that I probably wouldn't be having another for a few days, so it was important for me to feel clean. I'm sure most people wouldn't have bothered, but I have a thing about hygiene and if it was going to make me feel better then that's what I would do. Luckily, I also had time. It was at this point that I had my first experience of hospital underwear, when I was given some paper see-through nappy-like pants to wear!

At around 8 am the porter came to collect me and take me to theatre. This time I was allowed to walk in. It was the longest walk of my life. I was again taking in all my surroundings, and I walked all the way into the theatre room and climbed onto the bed myself. I remember asking how long it would be until

I was knocked out. 'About five seconds' was the reply.

Six to seven hours later the day was over and I awoke in critical care. It took a few seconds for me to come round and remember what I had been through, so much so I didn't want to move. I didn't even want to breathe, as I was petrified of the pain. However, lying there as still as I could, I realised that I really wasn't in too much pain. But then I was connected to various things and had had a local anaesthetic on top of the general, so I was probably still numb.

The only way I can really describe it is like a tightness in my stomach. I seemed to have so much stuff wrapped around my body that I felt as if I was being held together. My legs were raised quite a bit, so it became obvious that I would be unable to lie flat. I was also covered by what they call a 'bear hugger', which was to keep me warm.

I had what I believe was a morphine drip in my right hand. The nurses told me that if I started to feel any pain I should press the button. It wasn't long before I needed to do this, as when I took a deep breath or coughed, it hurt. However when I pressed the button a shooting pain shot through my hand. I thought I must have imagined it, so I did it again, but the pain was still there and it was worse than that in my stomach. I didn't do it again and neither did I tell any of the nurses. I didn't want them to think I was weak.

I lay there clock watching, and the minutes turned into hours. Some time later I started to really struggle each time I coughed, the pain was so bad. The nurse asked why I hadn't pressed the button and I finally told her. She said the needle might have been positioned slightly wrong. They could move it to the other hand if it bothered me, but it should still be working.

I then discovered that I needed to be able to cough comfortably before they would let me out of critical care, so with the option of yet another injection or just dealing with the pain, I chose the latter. I kept pressing the button until I couldn't feel anything any more.

My throat felt like sandpaper. I don't think I've ever drunk so much, although the nurses do limit the amount you can have. I remember being desperate for some lemon squash. I don't like water at the best of times, but that seemed to be all that was by my bed. One of the nurses kindly went off and got me some squash and I have never been so grateful.

I was also now starting to realise the extent of what I had been through. I was too scared to move and I knew I wouldn't be able to stand. I had no idea what would come next or how long I would be there for.

Through the night I had three different nurses looking after me and they were all great. I was really struggling to sleep, though. This was the beginning of my ongoing insomnia.

Friday 30th April

This morning the nurses told me I would be leaving critical care, but due to problems finding me a bed in the private ward, I had to go back to the main ward instead. I was devastated.

Maybe my feelings were enhanced by what I had been through, and I got upset. I couldn't face a ward. I didn't expect people to understand, I just wished it wasn't happening.

My surgeon came in to see me and luckily he understood why I was so upset. He was worried about me. He said he'd go and find out what was happening. I don't know how he did it, but he managed to get me a room and thankfully I never returned to the ward.

A couple of male nurses wheeled me to my room and sorted out getting my bags. Like any normal person, one of the first things I wanted was my phone, but I couldn't reach my bag and that was the point at which I realised just how little I could move. I was feeling quite upbeat, but then all of a sudden an overwhelming need to sleep hit me. It's amazing how much your body can withstand, and therefore not surprising how little energy you have. I wasn't awake for long.

In the evening I discovered that I would have to have another blood thinning injection. I wasn't expecting that, but apparently when you are in hospital you have one every night. I also had what resembled flight socks on, to stop blood clots caused by the lack of movement.

The nurse sorted out my bed for me. I had pillows under my legs and a remote control so I could elevate them further if I got uncomfortable. I don't know where the day went. I think I must have drifted in and out of sleep for most of it.

I was really anxious about the next morning. What would they make me do? I was feeling it would be impossible to get out of bed and I felt as if I could just lie there forever. The bed was now to become my comfort blanket.

Saturday 1ˢᵗ May

I discovered quite quickly that the aim was to get you up as soon as possible. Almost as soon as I was awake the nurse came in and removed my catheter. Little things like this freaked me out. The thought of having a balloon blown up in my bladder just didn't feel right, and I was petrified I'd feel them deflate it - I mean it's not natural to have something in your bladder! However, for the record, I didn't feel a thing. I was scared though, as I knew this meant I'd now have to get out of bed.

I had four drains in me, something I wasn't aware of before the operation, so it came as a bit of a shock. They are tubes which drain excess fluid from the wounds, leading to bottles which I had to carry around with me over the next few days. Two were inserted into my newly-constructed left breast and the other two into my stomach. To say I was nervous about moving would be an understatement. I convinced myself that I would feel them and panicked that I may drop them. However, I hadn't taken into account the fact that both the areas where they were inserted were completely numb.

The time now came to take my first tentative steps. I can't quite put into words the way I felt when I moved. It wasn't so much pain as fear. I could barely move, so the nurse gently lifted the drains to one side of the bed and then pulled my legs over, and slowly I twisted my body until I was sort of in a sitting up position. I couldn't stand up straight and my stomach was covered in weird-looking soft plastic or rubber stuff, which I thought at this point was stopping me from standing upright. The nurse helped me to walk very slowly to the bathroom, although to be fair it was more of a shuffle, as I was hunched over at an almost 90 degree angle.

There was no way I could stand, and I was thankful when I saw a seat in the bathroom. The nurse helped me briefly, but it was clear that the aim was to do it myself. At this point I was sitting half naked in the chair with barely enough energy to lift the sponge. It's amazing how you lose all your dignity in hospital, but really don't care!

I was now thinking that maybe I shouldn't drink too much, as there was no way I could keep getting up and down to use the bathroom.

I had my first visitors later that day. Teresa and Kez had come in to see me - Kez had come up from Devon for the weekend. Before I had gone into hospital, I was keen for a visit on the Saturday. I had no idea how weak I'd feel. It's weird, because you physically can't be bothered to speak, let alone entertain people, but it's hard when it's someone you haven't seen for a while, as you feel you need to talk. However, after a short conversation I was shattered. I had been sitting in a chair, but I shuffled back to my bed, then hardly said a word. I felt a bit guilty, but I really couldn't focus on talking. I just wanted to sleep.

It had been the same when people had phoned - I just couldn't find the energy to speak. I had texted everyone earlier to say the operation had gone fine and I was knackered. But when people texted back, I had to muster the energy to reply.

Sunday 2nd May

It was the bank holiday weekend and Kate came in for the first of her daily visits. It was easy with Kate, as I didn't actually have to speak. We just sat and watched the telly. I also found it amusing that she turned her nose up at anything I tried to show her or explain to do with my operation. I, on the other hand, was getting used to the drains, but was not looking forward to them being removed, not now I had discovered that they just pull them out!

The furthest I could walk was to the bathroom and back. Other than that I sat in my chair for most of the day. I was too scared to attempt walking anywhere. I figured that at some point I would see the physiotherapist and find out what I could and couldn't do. In the meantime, I would do nothing.

Monday 3rd May

In the early hours of the morning, I awoke having a coughing fit. My stomach didn't feel right and I was scared that when I coughed, the pressure would be too much for the wound and it would open up. I put my hand on my stomach in a protective gesture and felt something wet. My heart sank, but I tried not to panic. I turned the light on and slowly lifted the sheets. My pyjamas were covered in blood.

I lay there for a few seconds, not wanting to know where the blood was from, but then I pressed the call button, praying it wasn't bad. I wasn't in any pain, so I was trying to be realistic. It was probably just a small bit that had come open and it'd be fine.

A nurse came in and had a look. Thankfully it was fine, it wasn't the main wound but the place where one of the drains had been inserted. My coughing fit must have aggravated it. A simple clean-up by the nurse and help with changing my pyjamas, and I was back to sleep.

Throughout those nights in hospital, a nurse would make regular visits to check blood pressure, pulse and temperature, so you never really slept through an entire night. I also had regular checks of my breast to make sure everything was alive and not being rejected after the operation. They called it a flap, which always made me laugh, but all they had to do was put a piece of equipment on it which would show if it was healthy or not. Thankfully, I never had any issues.

In the morning a nurse came to see me and asked if I wanted to try having a shower. This was quickly followed by the realisation that I was in a room with a bath only! Luckily they now had another empty room with a shower, so they decided to move me.

Tessa and Kate came in to see me. I still wasn't really

moving about and the furthest I could go was a few feet down the corridor when I moved rooms.

The nurse checked on the drains to see if they were ready to come out. They decided that the two in my breasts were ready, but the other two would have to stay. They went off to get the equipment and the wait for them to come back seemed to go on forever. My heart was sinking and I started to panic. I just needed it to be over. I was so scared. I felt I couldn't breathe and I could feel the fear in the pit of my stomach. The thought of them pulling tubes out made me feel sick, and I was terrified about what I would feel.

When she returned, she removed the tape around the tube and told me to take some deep breaths. Then just as she was about to pull it out I had to breath in. I'm not really sure why she had told me to do that. As it turned out, I didn't really feel anything, which was probably because I was completely numb in that area, both the inside and outside of my breast. However, that didn't stop my stomach being in knots at the thought of going through it again in the morning.

After this I had to manage a shower without soaking my wounds too much. The rubber stuff covering them had been removed and I was left with tape - lots of it. I hadn't realised that I wasn't having stitches. I guess medical procedures have moved on somewhat, but I didn't feel too comfortable that my tummy was being held together by tape!

The shower wasn't too eventful, especially since I could barely move still. If anything it was hard work, although there was a chair in there, so I just sat and let the water run over me. I then barely had the energy to dry myself. I went from someone who normally wouldn't leave the house without showering to someone who couldn't care if they never showered again. It was too much like hard work!

Tuesday 4th May

The anticipation of having the stomach drains removed was there again. The butterflies were at full pelt and I was willing the time to hurry up so it would be over. The nurse kept coming in and out, getting things ready. Finally we were ready and again she told me to take a deep breath. The feeling this time as she pulled the drain out was indescribable. There was zero pain, but I hate anything remotely gruesome and as she pulled it out, I felt something inside my body moving, which made me feel sick. However it was quick, only seconds. She then said the other drain had to stay, as it wasn't quite ready, so onto another day of anticipation.

Kate came in again after work and we decided I needed to try moving, so we did a very slow walk up the corridor to the visitors' room. On the way back we passed a lady who had a tube in her neck. She spoke to us briefly and I wondered what she had gone through. I got a wave of realisation that I was in a cancer hospital and everything that had happened to me whirled around my brain. At times it still felt unreal, so seeing other people was like a reality check.

I remember stopping and leaning against the wall and

being overcome with the sense that I wasn't going to make it back to my room. I felt I desperately needed to sit down, but there were no chairs. I had to keep going, I couldn't give up. Finally we made it back.

In the evening two more friends came in and I was determined to keep trying to walk, as surely it must get better. We did another slow walk to the visitors' room. I felt I needed to keep doing this, as I was conscious that I was unable to stand upright and worried about coping at home. However I think I maybe overdid it, as when we get back I was shattered.

Wednesday 5th May

For the third morning in a row my stomach was in knots at the thought of the drain removal. Again I felt on the verge of a panic attack. The sensation as it came out was there again. Afterwards the nurse showed me how long the tube inside me was, which explained why I felt it come out! Thankfully it was now all over and I would never have to endure that again.

I was due to see the physiotherapist later and the plan was to go home the next morning. If I'm honest, I didn't want to go home. The hospital was my comfort and I felt I needed the staff to protect me. My surgeon had previously suggested I might be able to go home on the Tuesday, but I had said I wasn't ready. There was no way I would have coped with the drains at home. However I knew I couldn't keep saying that, as I would have to get used to the idea of leaving at some point.

When I got to see the physiotherapist, she suggested we try

some stairs. This was mainly because I would have to use the stairs at home, so I had to be able to manage them before leaving. We started by walking slowly to the front of the ward and out of the main doors to the corridor where the stairs were. By the time I reached them, I was already knackered and feeling nervous, as the stairs looked like a mountain and a very difficult one to climb.

With every step I took my energy was drained further. I was trying to cope with an inability to stand straight while lifting my foot, holding onto the rail and breathing. We went up one flight and then came back down. I can't believe how difficult such a simple task had become.

Later that day, I had my first outing to the hospital café. We made it out to the corridor and waited for the lift, but as we did so my energy levels dipped really low and I remember being desperate to sit down as I felt I was going to collapse. The lift seemed to take forever, but thankfully I didn't collapse and we made it down to the café and back again.

I looked a right state, but bizarrely was not too bothered. I guess clothes, hair and makeup were the least of my worries. It is interesting that when you are ill you don't have the energy to care what you look like, let alone to do something about it.

Thursday 6th May

In the morning, while I was waiting to be discharged, I had a conversation with a nurse who hadn't long been back from travelling. We got into a conversation about our dreams, one of mine being to go to Borneo and work with the orang-utans. I didn't believe this would ever happen, but I remember her saying I could do anything I wanted and not to miss out on things. This would ring true further down the line.

I was given a bag of various drugs for pain relief and very slowly made my way out of the ward with Claire, who had come to pick me up with her boyfriend Rob. However the walk through the hospital to the car was traumatic, as it seemed to go on forever and I really thought at times I wouldn't make it. I couldn't stop as there was nowhere to sit down and no wheelchairs in sight. I had to muster up all my energy just to get to the front doors, and was relieved when we finally got there, but I was now facing steps down to the car. I managed them, just, and collapsed very gratefully into the car.

As we drove home I realised how delicate I was. I was petrified of the car hitting a bump and hurting my stomach. Every time I saw a pothole or drain, or even when Rob put his foot on the brake, I clutched my stomach in anticipation of pain. I was thankful to arrive home and headed straight for the sofa. Today's events had again taken it out of me and all I wanted to do was sit and do nothing. Claire and Rob stayed for a short while, but I didn't feel overly sociable. I guessed this was the start of a long recovery.

Today was election day, and I was adamant that I would be going to put my vote in, which is strange since I hadn't voted since I was eighteen. At least I was adamant this time last week. We waited a few hours, then took a drive to the polling station and again every little jolt in the car filled me with dread and the need to clutch my stomach in a protective gesture.

When we arrived, I started to think it was a mistake. I hadn't counted on little things becoming such missions. It was starting to become clear that part of the healing process was about what goes on in your head and not just the actual pain. I looked at how far from the car I needed to walk and panicked slightly, and that was before I had even moved. I remember shuffling across the car park and as we got to the entrance I was convinced I would collapse.

Focus was the only word I can think of - focus on making it to the room and pray there are chairs in there. I was very aware that to look at there was nothing visibly wrong with me, so people would probably be wondering what was wrong with this strange girl who looks like she's doubled up in pain as she shuffles along. I made it, and clocked a seat by a piano, so I went straight over to it. I'm sure people were looking at me weirdly, but I didn't care. Sitting down was the only thing that mattered.

Once I had regained my strength, we made our way out. This time I waited on a seat outside while Kate brought the car to me.

CHAPTER FOUR

Over the next few days I barely moved. I honestly couldn't see an end to this. Would I ever be able to stand up straight again?

When I was in bed, I had to sleep with pillows or cushions under my legs as I couldn't lie flat. I kept trying to stretch out, but it was too painful. Just getting into bed was a mission in itself. I felt as if I was ninety. First I had to practically crawl up the stairs, followed by very slowly and tentatively sitting on my bed before getting my legs up and onto the pillows and very slowly lying back onto more pillows. How long I was going to be like this for was anyone's guess.

The physio had given me exercises, but this meant getting motivated. I was well aware that if I did nothing, I might not get full movement back and a year down the line would be too late, so I set my mind to it and started with one that was to gain me full movement in my arm again. At this point I could only raise it to a 90 degree angle in front of me; it felt impossible to get it any higher. I found this really hard, as I couldn't understand why I couldn't make my body do as I wanted. I felt I had no control. It was a bit like trying to bend something in the wrong direction - it wasn't so much pain as the simple inability to do it. If I tried to force it, it hurt.

I was also experiencing electric shock-like symptoms in my breast at night and it felt heavy. On the basis that it was numb, it was almost a relief to feel something. I kept getting an itch, either there or on my stomach, but the area where the itch was was numb, so it didn't make sense and I had to rub really hard to stop it.

At the weekend my dad, granddad, brother, sister-in-law and nephew came to visit me. We decided to go to the pub for lunch, which was nice as it meant me being able to get out, although I wasn't too sure how far I'd get. Getting from the car to the door was still a struggle, and I ended up using my nephew as a walking frame, which he seemed to like.

Tuesday 11th May

Today I had an appointment to see Mr Harris at his Portland Street consultancy. They don't make it easy, as I can barely walk and the thought of getting trains and tubes wasn't a happy one. In fact there was no way I'd be able to do it. I thought I'd have to get a taxi instead, but luckily I have friends who don't mind driving into central London and they came to my rescue.

The journey was horrendous and took us two hours. At least that meant we were going slowly, so I didn't have to clutch my stomach the whole way. When we arrived, we found a place to park and I shuffled across the street to a plush-looking building wondering if we were in the right place.

The consultancy suite was in this building and the waiting room was not what a normal waiting room looked like - it seemed very posh. There was a book on the surgeons who worked there and what procedures they carried out. I pointed out who my surgeon was and shortly after that I was called through.

I remember the nurse calling me in and me shuffling along the corridor saying 'I'm coming, might be a while, but I'm coming'. I was seriously starting to think I'd never be able to stand up straight again.

This was to be the first time I'd see my scars, and I was a little nervous. I already knew that the scar on my stomach was a lot higher than the bikini line, because my blood vessels were higher than expected. I also believe this was why some of my muscle had been cut, which I guess meant being able to do sit-ups would take a little longer than expected.

The nurse removed all the dressing. The main wound on my stomach had dissolvable stitches, which as I've previously said, scared me as I couldn't understand how I wouldn't just tear open. However, when I saw the scar I was happy to see that the wound had healed almost perfectly.

There was a little fluid about halfway along the scar, so Mr Harris asked me to stand up so he could remove it. I stood on the footstall to get onto the bed and saw to my horror that he had a syringe in his hand. I guessed at that point that it wasn't quite over and I would still be going through the trauma of needles.

He pushed the syringe into the part of the scar that was slightly open, and all I can say is that no matter how numb I thought I was, I most certainly felt it. I grabbed both his shoulder and the nurses and gripped really hard. I can't say that it actually hurt, it was perhaps just my fear of what he was doing taking over.

Thursday 13th May

Two days later I had an appointment with Mr Cummins at Parkside Hospital. I still wasn't driving, so Robert took me in. It started as a simple check up. I got undressed and he checked over the scarring on my stomach and breast, but then he broached the subject of chemotherapy. I had known it was coming.

The oncology hospital was only a few doors down the road and Mr Cummins wanted me to book an appointment straight away. He asked me to wait for a nurse so she could talk to me and give me some information before I left, so I went back out into the waiting room until she called me through. Once I was in the room with her, I was fighting to hold back the tears. I can barely remember what she said to me, but she did give me a phone number for breast care nurses I could talk to for support. However, I knew I would never call it.

Monday 17th May

Less then a week later I had my appointment with Mr Charles Lowdell, who was to become my oncologist. I went with Tess, as I knew I wouldn't take it all in and she would be more focused on getting the information, writing it all down and asking questions. I don't remember much of this meeting, as I spent most of it trying my hardest to hold back the tears. If I spoke I knew I would cry, so I figured it would be better to say nothing.

He had a printout which indicated the likelihood of the cancer returning. Apparently they put all your details into the computer and it works out the statistics. For me it was like an insurance policy. I didn't need chemotherapy to shrink a tumour, but they wanted me to have it to kill all the cells which might or might not turn into tumours. This is something they can't tell by scans, as cancer can return at any point, so to give me the best possible chance of this not happening they wanted to combine chemotherapy with a five-year course of a drug called Tamoxifen.

It's a lot to take in. But despite all this, I still didn't want chemo. I'd only ever seen or heard of bad things, and I didn't know how I'd deal with it all.

Then came the news that really ripped my heart out. I was told that my ovaries would probably switch off during chemo and during the five years of taking Tamoxifen. Because of my, age it was unlikely they would switch back on. In short, I might go through the menopause, and it was unlikely I'd be able to have children.

All I had ever wanted was to settle down and have a family, though this might not have been obvious to those around me with the lifestyle I led. So here I was now at thirty-seven, regretting every decision I'd ever made in my life. If I hadn't gone travelling when I was younger, or had actually made the effort to settle down, I wouldn't be in this position. I had single-handedly ruined my own chances of ever having a family, and there was jack shit I could do about it. I had sealed my own fate.

My cancer was hormone related, so the option of freezing eggs was not recommended, as whatever process they use to do this could actually feed any cancer. Eggs also need to be fertilized, and I'm single, so that's not going to happen.

I didn't want it, it was that simple. I didn't want it. My brain was working on overdrive. I wanted to have the courage to say no, but I said nothing. Dr Lowdell explained that we needed to start as soon as possible, which meant I could be having treatment this time next month.

I didn't make a decision then and there, as obviously I had a lot to think about, so we went home. I could still barely have a conversation about how I really felt at this point, as I would have just burst into tears if I did. I have never felt so alone in all my life. I wanted someone to tell me what to do or to tell me it was all going to be OK, but no one could do that.

At some point I'd have to snap out of it and make the decision. I knew if I said no I'd be living the rest of my life in fear, and I knew that if the cancer returned people would automatically say it was because I turned the chemo down. Though it might come back anyway, so I guess I'd never really know.

I spoke to many people about what they thought and they all said it was my decision, but it was obvious that they all thought I shouldn't turn the chemo down. Even when they said they understood, they didn't, how could they?

It was some harsh words from my brother that made my mind up. I was upset that I might never be able to have children and he told me straight that it would be a lot worse if I did and then died, leaving them motherless. Thanks bro!

Thursday 20th May

This was going to be a long day, as I was having a full-body bone scan. This consisted of an injection in the morning, which I believed was yet another radioactive liquid direct into my vein to show up any abnormalities before we went onto the actual scan, where a machine moves slowly over you (fully clothed) and takes pictures. The problem was that I had to wait a few hours after the injection to have the scan, and because I wasn't driving, that essentially meant spending all day at the hospital. Thankfully, again, Kate dropped me off in the morning and then came back at lunchtime prior to the actual scan.

I remember it being a really beautiful day, so rather than sitting in the hospital between scans we decided on taking a short walk to Wimbledon Common. I was shuffling about a lot better now. I still couldn't stand straight, but I was slowly building up my walking ability.

We were planning on sitting in the fields somewhere while we waited for the next scan, which would have been good as I was starting to struggle. However, after an unsuccessful search to find some rabbit-poo-free grass we gave up and headed back to the hospital.

Once we found the place where we needed to be, we sat and waited until finally an Australian male doctor called me through. As I got up, Kate casually pointed out a caterpillar on my leg. I doubt she expected the reaction she got. My brain must have been on overload, and without even looking or acknowledging what it was, I did a really pathetic scream, started jumping up and down and begged the doctor to get it off. He looked slightly scared, but obliged.

Once that little drama was over, I went into the room for the scan. I was always slightly nervous as I still couldn't lie down flat and I was worried that that is what I would have to do. Luckily, and probably obviously, they always seemed to know I was in discomfort, and they automatically helped me onto the bed and put pillows under my legs.

As with most of the scans I have had that involve liquid of some sort being injected into me, I was told to drink lots of water afterwards to stop it collecting in my bladder.

Wednesday 26th May

A few things of importance started today. Firstly, I decided to start driving again. Maybe a little prematurely, but I couldn't keep asking my friends for lifts and the hospital was too far away for taxis. Secondly, since I had made the decision to go ahead with chemotherapy, I was going to meet the nurses and have a tour of the chemotherapy unit. Finally I was getting the results of the scan. I was a little nervous, as I was guessing it would show up any issues still lurking.

I took a slow and very cautious drive to the hospital, avoiding bumps at all costs. It wasn't too bad. I guess that four weeks after the operation the problem was more in my mind than really hurting. The main reason I wanted to get back in my car was to get over this.

Apparently I had a couple of abnormalities, which had shown up from the scans. However, it is worth noting that if anyone who has no hospital records of previous scans has a scan, there is a likelihood that something will show up. In short he told me it was normal and not to worry.

The abnormalities that had come to light were a gallstone, which was rather large, and a shadow on my lungs. He said he would do another scan in about six months to see if anything had changed, but it was likely to just be scarring of some sort, which would make sense as I had had pleurisy five years previously. The gallstone could just be ignored, but I should let them know if I had any pain.

Things had moved on really quickly, and we had agreed my course of chemotherapy, which was to start on June 2nd, then once every three weeks for six sessions. He had scheduled the start date so as not to ruin my forthcoming holiday on the 13th June, as ideally by then I would be in a good week on the side effect front. He had explained that the side effects were different for everyone. The normal experience would be that in week one I probably wouldn't feel well, week two my blood counts would increase, so I should start feeling better, and week three I should feel fine. Then the cycle starts again.

After our chat we went downstairs to the chemotherapy unit and I was introduced to a lady called Julie, who would explain the whole process to me. As expected, it was a little daunting. I had been taken to a room which was full of literature on cancer, chemotherapy, how to cope etc etc, and to top it off, there was a nice display of wigs in the corner. As I sat there my eyes scanned the room. It was one of those times when I didn't want to look, but at the same time I did want to look, if that makes any sense!

I remember feeling really tearful, but trying so hard to hide it. I couldn't ask the questions I really wanted to ask, as every time I opened my mouth I welled up, so as usual I gave up and just listened to what Julie had to say. Not that I can share any of what I was told on that day, as I have no idea - not because it didn't make sense, but because I was too upset to take anything in, and being told about something doesn't compare to actually doing it.

I then had one of my 'didn't see this one coming' moments, when I was told I needed to have a blood test before chemotherapy. I think it was to show them my current blood count levels. Whatever the reason, I wasn't too happy and launched into a full account of my fear of needles. Luckily, she was one of the most understanding nurses I have ever met and promised to be gentle and get it right the first time. However as usual, it didn't work, that wasn't predicted! She had to try again, but to be fair, it wasn't too painful.

One of the things we spoke about was having a thing called a portacath, which is a tiny plastic tube inserted into a vein under the skin in your chest. This would be where the chemotherapy would be administered and would be easier and a lot less painful then being injected every week. However, at this point I didn't really understand and believed I would have a tube sticking out of my chest. Because of this and the fact that I was going on holiday, I had declined it. However she told me it was a much easier way of administering chemotherapy, so I agreed to have one fitted on my return, prior to my second dose.

CHAPTER FIVE

Wednesday 2nd June

The day had finally arrived for chemotherapy to begin. I felt strange going to the oncology hospital - I'm not sure I had quite got my head around the fact that I was about to go through chemotherapy. I think it's the not knowing that is the worst, not knowing what they'll do, not knowing if it will hurt, not knowing if you'll be ill. They had explained everything previously, but it doesn't make it any easier. You just have to wait and deal with whatever is thrown at you.

Fiona and Kate came with me for my first session. When we arrived we were shown to a large room, which had wooden partitions. They were a bit like dressing partitions, separating all the people from one another to give you a bit of privacy. We had the choice of a few places to sit, so I picked a place in the corner by a window. We took our seats, me on the biggest one that reclined - and then they came and took our order for lunch! None of us was expecting that.

The first thing I had to do was to have a blood test. They do this before every session, and because I had declined having the port inserted prior to my holiday they had to do this through my hand again. The nurse seemed to have a way of getting my veins visible by using warm water. She struggled though, and when it was finally done she said she had used a baby needle and that I had crooked veins! At least that's something I could say in the future to anyone attempting to inject me.

I had also decided I wanted to try a procedure called scalp cooling. This is a system used to reduce hair loss during chemotherapy. The way it works is by freezing your scalp to about minus 4, which causes the blood vessels which supply the hair follicles to shrink. This means that less of the chemotherapy drug reaches the follicles. There is a risk however that by doing this, you are not killing all your cells, which is the whole point of chemotherapy, however the risk is so small it wasn't worth the worry.

I had been advised to have my hair cut short before chemo, but I couldn't go through with it. I honestly believed that the more hair I had the less chance I would have of losing it. You need to understand that at this point you really can't imagine losing your hair and will truly believe that the scalp cooling will work. It's like anything else - seeing is believing and until it happens, it's hard to believe.

For the scalp cooling to have any effect, they need to start it about half an hour prior to the chemo and then continue for about half an hour at the end. I was using a cap attached to a machine, which meant I couldn't move about unless they detached it. The unit was already by my chair and there was what looked like a hard cap covered in ice. The nurse removed all the ice, then gently fitted it onto my head. She then covered it with a fabric cap and turned the unit on.

I can honestly say, that for the first ten minutes I was close to quitting. It is a pain I can't even begin to describe. Imagine holding a few bags of frozen peas against your head, or that head freeze we sometimes experience when eating ice cream, only you don't know when it's going to stop. I had read that it was painful for the first ten minutes, but as with most things, you can't really comprehend it until you are personally feeling it. Within ten minutes however, your head goes numb and you can no longer feel the coldness, so it's worth persevering.

At the start of my session and after we had debated the correctness of whether we should take photos in a chemotherapy hospital or not (I wish I had now), I settled into a focused frame of mind, attempting to think of anything but the cap on my head. I really didn't want to look as if I was uncomfortable, and I didn't want a bit of pain to beat me. So I persevered with it, and sure enough after about ten minutes my head went numb, to the point when I was convinced it had warmed up. I kept touching it and pushing it harder onto my head until I could feel the coldness again.

A little while later the chemo was due to start. This had to be administered by hand, rather than a bag, which as I have previously said was because I had not had a port fitted. They put a cannula into a vein in my hand and this was used to insert the drugs. There were so many different things, but the first was to give me anti-sickness tablets and I believe another version of these went through the cannula.

I was having a combination called FEC, which is made up of three different drugs, Fluorouracil, Epirubicin and Cyclophospamide. They took about half an hour each. The first was a red liquid - I remember looking at it and thinking I couldn't believe this was going into my body and the damage it would be doing. The other two were clear liquids. I also had a saline drip connected throughout, which I believe was to keep me hydrated.

I remember being fascinated by my surroundings, almost in disbelief that I was even there. Looking around the room, I could see some patio doors, which were slightly ajar. Outside was a small courtyard and the sun was shining. What a way to start the summer.

Inside by the doors was a magazine rack and a fruit basket. I guess there's no harm in trying to be healthy at this point!

I started to ask about the portacath again and what it looked like when a lady came over and showed me hers. It wasn't as horrific as I had imagined - there was no tube sticking out of her skin. What I saw on that day was after the tube had been connected. It's a small, almost square and quite flat-looking object with what looks like a needle on the end, I didn't really understand how it connected, but somehow they connect the tubes giving the chemo to this port. It didn't look too bad, so I was comfortable about having it inserted once our holiday was over.

The lady looked as if her hair had been growing for a few months, although I couldn't understand how, if she was still going through chemo. I would never know the answer to that.

Perhaps she had been unfortunate and the cancer had returned, or perhaps her hair had started regrowing during chemo. She never said and I never asked.

When it was all over, they gave me a bag of drugs to take home. They said I would need to return 24 hours later to have an injection to boost my white blood cells; this is done after every chemotherapy session. Apparently you can administer this at home to save you from having to come back, but just the suggestion of that was met with a nervous laugh from me. That was just never going to happen.

I was staying in the hospital overnight, which is standard after the first session in case of serious side effects. The two hospitals, the oncology hospital where I had chemotherapy, and Parkside, where I would be staying overnight, were within walking distance. I was still having trouble walking though, so we opted for the car

I had a few visitors to keep me company, but by 9.30 pm I had started to feel extremely nauseous, and everyone left so I could try to sleep. The nurse told me to take some anti-sickness tablets and lie down. I did this and the nausea eventually passed. I was also hooked up to a saline drip for the night.

Thursday 3rd June

After leaving Parkside I returned to the oncology hospital for my injection. They usually do this in a fatty part, like your stomach. I was keen to do this, as I was convinced my stomach was numb, so I wouldn't feel anything. What I hadn't counted on was that it's not the injection that hurts but the liquid that is released. I nearly hit the roof. I remember grabbing hold of the sides of the chair. Maybe having had all the fat removed from my stomach made it more painful. Whatever the reason, I swore I would never have an injection in that part of my body again.

I was due to go on holiday the following Sunday, so I was told I would have to return for a blood test before going. This was because chemotherapy can lower your resistance to infection. I was told my white blood cell count might drop, which would leave me open to infection.

I then went home and for the next two days I was wiped out with tiredness. I knew fatigue was a side effect, but I had that and insomnia as well. The only other effects I experienced after this first session were the entire inside of my mouth turning white, which lasted about a week, and my taste buds going a bit haywire, which for someone who doesn't eat well at the best of times wasn't good.

My energy slowly came back, but since I was still struggling to stand up straight and carry anything I just lay on my sofa for the best part of the next week and continued with my arm and stomach excercises.

Thursday 10th June

I drove myself back to Parkside for my blood test. Not in a million years did I believe anything would be wrong, but when I arrived I was told that my haemoglobin levels were very low, which meant my immune system was low, leaving me open to infection. It's strange, because at this point I really couldn't imagine getting ill, even after all I had been through. It was as if my subconscious would only let me believe I was ill when I was in some sort of pain, and until then I was fine and yet again indestructible. I got a horrible feeling that they were going to tell me I couldn't go, but they decided to give me some antibiotics to take on holiday, only to be taken in an emergency. They also printed out my blood test results to take with me, just in case I did need to go to hospital. They made sure I understood what to look out for and to check my temperature. I think it was a close call with them allowing me to fly.

Saturday 12th June

We had a barbecue today to celebrate Kate's birthday and I was feeling OK for the most part, but when *Just Dance* was put on the Wii I made my excuses. After all, I was still only about six weeks away from having my stomach cut open!

I started to struggle late in the evening, and although I still wasn't sleeping, I was shattered. I couldn't take a sleeping tablet though, as we had an early start to the airport. The party continued downstairs and I had to try my best to block out the noise.

Sunday 13th June

Today seven of us flew to Portugal for our week's holiday. At this point, to any onlooker, there was nothing wrong with me, nothing visible to say I was ill, but I felt extremely tired the whole time. I was still unable to stand completely upright as there was still a pulling sensation on my stomach. I couldn't carry anything heavy, but luckily Kate was on hand to pull my suitcase.

Although I was really looking forward to the holiday, I was also very worried; I didn't want to ruin it for everyone else if I couldn't do things. I figured I would just try and be strong and not let the chemo get the better of me.

Every night I was shattered. I didn't want to go to bed if everyone else was staying up, but my body was telling me I didn't have much choice. Nearly every night I took a sleeping tablet, as no matter how tired I was I still couldn't sleep.

Luckily the holiday turned into one of those relaxing weeks where you don't do much and stay in the villa most of the time. I struggled only in the evenings. If we went out it tended to be after seven and we would eat later, yet I would have happily been tucked up in bed by ten.

I have always worn bikinis on holidays and didn't want this year to be any different, but I was very self consious of my scarring and the fact that I now looked slightly abnormal in terms of my body shape, as I also had a load of fat sitting on my hips. However I had been given some of the tape they had used on my stomach and it was almost skin coloured, so I now had a daily ritual of putting the tape over the scar. This also protected it from the sun and held down the fat on my hips. It seemed to do the job and I felt a lot less worried about what I looked like.

Because I had had lymph nodes removed, I had been told I was at risk of a condition called lymphoedema. This in short is a swelling caused by a build-up of lymph fluid, which would be on my arms since the lymph nodes were in my armpit. It's the sort of thing that can occur straight away or years down the line. From my understanding, once you have it, there is no cure, but it can be controlled. I was advised not to carry heavy weights on that arm or go into hot tubs, and I guess this will be forever. It was a shame, as there was a nice hot tub in our villa's outside area by the pool. I did sit in it briefly, but was petrified of developing this illness, as there would be no hiding a swelling.

Everything went fine until the Monday evening, when I had a shower and some of my hair visibly came out. It wasn't so much in clumps, more like a lot of strands all at once. When I brushed my hair the entire brush would become full and I seemed to be putting rather a lot in the bin. I didn't say anything at first, but every day it got worse and worse until I was filling carrier bags up with all my hair. I finally got Kate to come into my bathroom and take a look at the amount I had lost. By the night before we came home it was impossible for me to use a hairdryer, and when I ran the straighteners through my hair it just stuck to them. When I took a shower, I became covered in hair. It was frustrating, as well as slightly traumatic.

I was devastated. Luckily at this point it wasn't noticeable, as I had thick hair. In fact the amount that came out before it did become noticeable was unbelievable. It's hard to put into words how I was feeling. I felt no one could understand, especially as at that point other people couldn't really see it. The support I had was phenomenal, but I still felt the whole world was against me. I still felt very alone. I just wanted to sound off about it non-stop to everyone, but I knew I couldn't do that as it would annoy people. It wasn't supposed to happen like this. I had been told hair loss starts after the second or third dose, not twelve days after the first!

The pain eats away at you inside, but there's nothing you can do and I was on holiday and was pissed off that this had happened now. I was trying so hard not to let it bring me down. However, this was the first time since the chemo had started that I really cried.

Wednesday 16th June

Today didn't finish off the best for me. I was getting really frustrated in the evening before we went out, and I didn't even know why. I was just getting angry over everything and anything. My hair was coming out massively, and I figured that if this continued I'd be bald before we went home. This was the last night I tried to use the straighteners.

When we got back to the villa we all started to play Scrabble, but I went to bed after a while as I was shattered. As always I just lay there, completely unable to fall asleep. To make things worse, the soundproofing in the villa wasn't great and I felt I was still in the room playing Scrabble with them.

No one was being noisy, but I was getting angry all the same. I guess the lack of sleep was making me that way.

Friday 18th June

I threw a bit of a strop the next morning, because I was pissed off that I had been kept awake the previous night, which was pretty selfish since we were on holiday and I couldn't sleep anyway. Unfortunately I couldn't control how I was feeling at that time; I think it was because I was bottling everything else up. It was the little things that were making me snap.

All I could think was that I would probably have no friends left by the time we got home. I could only hope that they understood that this just wasn't really me.

We headed down to the harbour and a few of us went on a boat trip. Luckily the sight of the two crewmen on the boat took my mind off of being ill for a while! We were sneakily trying to take photos of them and I certainly believe I got the best shots.

The next day we flew home from Portugal and I began a nervous wait for my return to hospital on the Monday.

Monday 21st June

I had to be at the hospital for 7 am, as this was the day I was having the portacath put in. Tess picked me up on her way to work and dropped me off, which I was grateful for as I was staying overnight and had been advised not to drive the next morning.

This was to become my worst day, with needles the whole time. It started with a simple blood test. Three different nurses and five attempts later, they still hadn't managed it. At one point they gave up with my arm and tried my foot. I had never had an injection in my foot before and for some reason believed it would be fine, but no, as she put the needle in I felt an undescribable pain shoot through it. I literally screamed at her to stop. She pulled the needle out and said it might have hit a nerve. That area of my foot had a tingling sensation every time I touched it for about the next six weeks.

The doctor came in and explained the procedure to me. We had decided that the port would go in my chest, just above my right breast. There would be a small incision where the port would go and a tube would run up my neck slightly, which might be visible, and there would be a small scar at the top of this. I didn't really understand that part, but I was OK with it.

I was taken down to the room just outside the theatre and since it was now my third general anaesthetic of the year I decided to make a conscious effort to try and remember at what point I fell asleep. This didn't do me much good though, as I remember being told to stop fighting it. And then, once again, it was all over.

The operation went well. Afterwards, however, I kept touching my chest as I found it weird having this hard object under my skin and wanted to press on it, but at the same time was almost too scared to touch it in case it hurt. It grossed me out a bit, particularly when I noticed that if I turned my neck I could see the outline of a tube! I'm not too sure where it led to, as I didn't fully undertand what was inside me. At a guess though, I would imagine it went to a vein.

Wednesday 23rd June

I had now reached my second day of chemotherapy and the last three weeks seemed to have flown by. Other than feeling a bit down and having no energy, I wasn't really ill, so I was quite upbeat about today. My chest was still bruised from Monday's operation and the nurse did tell me that it might hurt a bit when they connected me up, but they had cottoned onto my fear of needles, so they put some numbing cream on me first.

I was petrified, as although I had seen my fellow patient's previously, I had only seen it connected. I thought I would have an exposed tube that was covered up with dressing, making the connection easy, but the port is actually beneath your skin and they have to pierce the skin to get to it. I braced myself in the chair as I now realised what the needle on the end of the square thing was about to do!

I was told to take a deep breath as they pierced my skin. Unfortunately it didn't go in and they had to try again. I think my port was on a bit of an angle, but they managed to get it in the second time and then took my blood, as again a blood test was the first part. I then had to go and see the oncologist before the chemotherapy started.

Despite quite a bit of hair thinning, I still decided to go

ahead with the scalp-cooling again and this time the first ten minutes weren't nearly as bad. When the blood results were back they unhooked me from the cooling unit, but I had to keep the cap on to go upstairs for my check up with the oncologist. I have never felt so self-conscious in all my life. I looked a joke walking around with this funny-looking cap on! But the oncologist needed to talk to me about any side effects I had experienced over the last three weeks so he would know if the correct dose was being given, as this can be changed if necessary.

I had been given a little red book, a bit like a diary where I was supposed to record everything (not that that happened!) but I remembered most, as I didn't think it was that bad. So I sat and explained that the only effects I had had were nausea on day one, but none since, tiredness and energy levels affected badly and diarrhoea for a couple of days. I had also experienced quite bad hot flushes. Apparently, all this was normal, so I then returned downstairs and they started the chemo.

This time it was in bags on a unit and injected through the port. The nurses could leave it to run its course; it notifies them by alarm if something's wrong. Again it took about 20 minutes per bag. It was so surreal being there, hooked up to a drug which effectively could be saving my life.

I had also previously been told that I could get a number of complimentary therapies throughout all this, so I had booked half an hour of reflexology, which I would definitely recommend. It was nice having it done whilst I was sitting there, as it took my mind off it all and helped relax me.

When the chemo had finished, thankfully I felt fine and was fully capable of driving myself home. I left with another bag full of drugs and agreed a time to return the next day for my injection.

After a few hours at home, I again became very lethargic and basically lacked any energy, so here I was again for a long stint on the sofa.

Thursday 24th June

As with last time, I felt completely wiped out, but I had to go back for my injection. When I got there I took a seat and a conversation about the cooling cap started, when a nurse said something about the lady sitting across the room. I started talking to her and it turned out that her Dad had worked for the same company as me. That was the first time I really spoke to anyone for any period of time in the hospital.

The moral of the story was that the cap doesn't really work, but I was still going to try. I was starting to panic a bit though, as I had a wedding on the Saturday and the only way I could cover my bald patches up was to constantly have my hair in a pony tail. With the rate it was coming out, I didn't think it would last till then.

Saturday 26th June

It was my cousin's wedding and this would be the furthest I had driven since this all started. I was praying I'd make it. I hadn't confirmed if I'd be going or not, as it was only three days after chemo and I really didn't know how I'd feel. However today I felt OK, so I decided I would go but just not stay late.

I also decided to wear my headscarf for the first time, which I was dreading, but I had decided that my hair was looking crap, so I had to do something. I felt a bit like a Romanian gypsy, in my dress and pink headscarf, but it was better than the alternative.

As we sat waiting for the ceremony, I tried to explain to my nephew why I had dressings and bruising on my chest. At six years old he was too young to understand, but he was very accepting of what I told him. We never dressed it up or hid anything, we just told him that I had been ill and was now having medicine to make me better, which was making my hair fall out. I let him touch the lump on my chest and explained that that was where the medicine was put. He didn't seem fazed.

I managed to stay until around 9 pm before I started to feel really tired. Luckily I was staying at Teresa's house about half an hour away, so although I was tired, I didn't have far to go. In the morning we were heading to a theme park to watch Pink in concert, in fact I had a long week as we had booked three concerts in ten days. I guess that wasn't the cleverest thing to do a few days after chemotherapy, but there was one thing I was always determined about, and that was that it wouldn't beat me.

Sunday 27th June

Gary, Teresa and I set off quite early, as we wanted to get up there to find a pub to watch the World Cup in, as England were playing. The only problem was that everyone and his mother seemed to have the same idea, so after trying a couple, we checked on line to see if they were playing it anywhere actually in the theme park. Thankfully we discovered that you could go and watch it on a big screen inside the grounds for £15 a head, so off we headed.

When we got to the park entrance we headed straight to the information centre, as I had called up in advance to ask if we could have seats on the disabled platform, because I couldn't stand for long periods and couldn't risk being crushed. On the phone it was simple - all I had to do was obtain a letter from my surgeon, which I did, and show it once I got there, which I did, but on the day I was met with blank faces. In fact it was the most complicated situation I found myself in and I certainly wasn't expecting the hassle. We got sent to two different places to try and sort it out, until finally they agreed, very reluctantly, to give us wristbands for the area.

Once in the park it was disorganised chaos. They did have the football on, but it was in a small area and the queues to get in were horrendous. I was petrified of getting crushed, as I still had issues with my stomach. People were starting to get irritated, as the queues were held back and only a few people were being let in at a time. We were finally let in after missing at least 15 minutes of the first half. For anyone who remembers that match, you'll understand when I say we didn't stay to watch the final score.

After the football we headed straight to the area where Pink was playing and found our way to the disabled platform. After all the initial hassle, the guy standing there happily let all three of us up without any fuss.

Friday 2nd July

Today was the second of our concert tour, as Teresa and I headed to the wireless festival in Hyde Park. I knew there was going to be a lot of walking involved, so I was a little worried. After the fiasco at the theme park, I wondered if we would actually get on the disabled platform without any problems. More so as I hadn't managed to contact them in advance to book anything.

The walk to find the park entrance we needed seemed to go on forever, but when we finally found it the staff couldn't have been more helpful. I knew it was touch and go with the seating and it was going to take a lot of luck, but they guaranteed me a space and said that if it was full Teresa could sit in front. However if we came back later they would check confirmed numbers and hopefully give us both wristbands. So off we went.

It was a relaxing day, as for the most part we were lying on the grass watching the acts. I had a bit of a bad time later though, when I started feeling nauseous and had to take some anti-sickness tablets for the first time, which was a bit depressing as I thought I'd got away with it. I then started to develop stomach cramps, so as it was getting nearer to the time for the evening performances we headed back to the entrance to check on the wristband situation. Thankfully they gave us both one, so we went to find our seats on the platform, which I was thankful for. However as the evening went on my stomach cramps were getting worse and I was longing to be at home.

As the concert came to an end we made a move to try and beat the crowds, but we didn't get too far before I needed to sit down as the pain in my stomach was becoming unbearable and my energy levels had gone to zero. I guess that this is where I should probably have listened to that little voice that says 'don't overdo it'.

By the time we got to the entrance to the tube station, the crowds were huge. We seemed to be in a surge of people and I was starting to get stressed. We decided to bypass it and try for a taxi on the street. Unfortunately a lot of other people had the same idea and we were getting nowhere fast. I have no idea how I managed to stay on my feet, as I was in agony. We seemed to be walking forever, although in reality it was not far, but it was taking everything in me not to just curl up in a ball on the pavement.

We found another tube station, but it was too packed for me to risk getting on a train with all the crushing. Finally we managed to hail a cab. Nightmare over!

Tuesday 29th June

Kez came to pick me up, as we were heading to Ipswich for the final concert. As I have already said, this was a full-on week for me and I was starting to feel the strain. You could say I had probably planned too much for one week. Again we had to find a different entrance from everyone else, as we had organised some seats. We ended up sitting on the pavement in the sunshine for a while first.

I didn't seem to have any problems this time, I was just extremely tired. I had recently started experiencing a new side effect, although I hadn't yet mentioned it to the doctor; my bones seemed to be aching and it all seemed to be in my back.

Tuesday 13th July

This was to be my last session of the FEC cocktail, as I would be on a new drug called Docetaxel for the final three sessions. I had my usual blood test and went to see Dr Lowdell before we started. I had asked for the cooling cap again, as despite the thinning I was still in denial. However, after one nurse had said yes, one of the older ones came along and advised me against it, as it clearly wasn't working and I was prolonging the trauma. Also, because of the cold, it would likely stick to my hair and pull it out when they took it off, so in some respects that would be worse. I reluctantly agreed to go without, as in my heart I knew she was right.

As I was hooked up to the drug, I suddenly became really light-headed. This was the first time I had experienced anything out of the ordinary while actually undergoing the chemo. I wondered if it was because my head had previously been frozen, stopping the chemo getting to certain places, whereas this time it felt as if it was going straight to my head.

I had reflexology again, which was relaxing. Once it had finished I was given my usual bag full of drugs to take home, except I now seemed to have a hell of a lot more. I had two different anti-sickness ones to take for the next three days plus a week's worth of capsules for my mouth infection, along with two different mouthwashes, painkillers and diazepam, which is a muscle relaxant and is supposed to help with sleep. I had more sleeping tablets and tablets for constipation. Finally there were the steroids for before my next session. I would start to feel as if I was jangling with pills soon!

Saturday 17th July

Today I realised that I had no photos of any of my wounds. I don't know why, it's one of those weird things where I feel I need an account of what has happened. My mum used to do it when we were kids. If my brother broke a bone, out the camera would come! So I guess I've got this from her and so today would be when I first started my photographic account.

In terms of side effects, I was starting to know what to expect:

- Chemo day, OK until later in the day when I feel tired.

- Two to three days of constipation, followed by a few days of diarrhoea.

- Approximately five days of the inside of my mouth turning completely white and everything tasting grim.

- Ongoing insomnia.

- Energy levels dropping in week one, but then get better in week two.

- Week three mainly fine, although still very tired.

The only thing I can't determine is the bone pain. This time round it seems to be getting worse, it has moved to my legs as well as my back and is bringing me to tears overnight as I just can't get comfy.

Wednesday 4th August

Last night the pain was unbearable. The only way I can describe it is like spasms, but constant and extremely painful. It was really weird, as I was only getting them at night. I couldn't lie on my front, I couldn't lie on my back and I couldn't curl up. It only started to subside if I got up and sat on the sofa, and even then it didn't completely go. As soon as I went back to bed, it got worse again. So most nights I spent awake, willing the pain to stop.

I had also started to take my water bottle to bed and would lie with it on my back, hoping it would relax the muscles so they wouldn't go into spasms, I think this may have helped a bit, but once it went cold the pain was back.

Today was the first session with the new drug. After reading about the side effects I was getting a little worried about the bone pain, as it wasn't listed for the FEC but I still got it. It was however listed with this one. Surely it couldn't get any worse. At least the end was getting near, as I only had two more sessions to go.

I spoke to them about my pain as it was becoming unbearable, so they gave me some liquid morphine to take overnight. The doctor said it was unusual to experience it overnight, but it seemed that when I started to sleep, my muscles relaxed, then went into spasm, which clearly then woke me up. I was beginning to wish for different side effects.

I had my usual reflexology during the session, which I would recommend as it is relaxing. For the most part I just sat there reading. At the end of the session I was given yet another bag of drugs. I was starting to look at them in disbelief as I couldn't believe how many pills and liquids I had to take.

I had Domperidone, which is an anti-sickness drug, and I took eight a day for three days. I took two Granisetron, another anti-sickness drug, a day for three days. Lansoprazole protects the stomach and I took one tablet daily until they had gone. I took two Diclofenac, an anti–inflammatory and painkiller, per day. Diazepam is a muscle relaxant and I could pretty much take these as and when required up to three times a day. Then there was Fluconazole for the mouth infection, which I needed for seven days, and Nystatin mouthwash, for the same thing, to be used for five days. Biotene mouthwash was to prevent mouth sores, and this was ongoing four times a day. Oramorph liquid is the liquid morphine for pain, to be taken as and when required – it smelt like the Calpol the kids use!

There were Zopliclone sleeping tablets and finally Docusate sodium capsules for constipation. Even with all these, I still needed to go back in the morning for the usual injection (Pegfilgrastim) 24 hours later to protect the white blood cells. I also had something called Dexamethasone, which is an anti-sickness steroid, which had to be taken two days before the next chemotherapy session. So just a few drugs!

Friday 6th August

I wasn't feeling good today. I was starting to get a sore throat and now and again had a bit of a stomach ache. I brushed it off though, as we were driving to Colchester for a friend's wedding the following day and I assumed it would pass.

It was a slightly longer drive than anticipated, as there was an overturned lorry on the Dartford crossing. I was willing the traffic to disperse so we could hurry up and get there, as for the whole journey I kept getting bouts of cramp, which had progressed somewhat from the stomach ache. I thought it would pass, so tried my best to ignore it.

When we got there, I wasn't feeling too bad and stayed up chatting for quite a while, but by the time I went to bed my stomach ache was permanently cramping and my throat was getting progressively worse. I lay down and prayed I wouldn't feel like this in the morning.

Saturday 7th August

I woke up after what I believed to have been a few minutes' sleep, and the stomach cramps were still there and getting worse. I had the hot water bottle I had been using to help with bone pain, but tonight it didn't seem to be helping with anything. So I lay in bed, willing the hours to pass and hoping for the pain to ease. However when morning finally came, it didn't show any sign of subsiding, so I figured I'd just have to grin and bear it.

To add to my trauma, as we started to get ready, my eyelashes decided to start falling out. They could have picked a better day! I knew it was going to happen, but I was just hanging onto the hope that it wouldn't. They didn't all come out in one go - it was more like when you pull false eyelashes off. I could have pulled them off in one big strip. I was devastated, but after staring in the mirror for a few minutes I left them alone, hoping that it would take longer for them to fall out if I didn't touch them. Luckily I had some false ones with me, although they were so big I began to wonder if bald was better!

When we got into the car the cramps seemed to get worse. I just didn't know what to do with myself and I wasn't linking the sore throat and the cramps together, I just made the assumption that I had some sort of tummy bug. I was conscious of what I had been told about my immune system dropping after chemo, but I think because I was absolutely fine after the first lot I couldn't imagine anything going wrong.

I felt really bad, as when we got to the wedding I was asked if I would be able to do a reading as the person doing it was running late. I refused, saying I couldn't stand up in front of everyone through shyness. It wasn't really a lie, but the real reason was that I was in so much pain that I physically couldn't have stood up anyway. I was just about getting away with sitting down.

Throughout the vows I was in absolute agony and was trying so hard to keep my focus on what was going on around me instead of the pain. When the ceremony was over we headed to the hotel for the meal, but I was desperate to get away from everyone, to lie down, sit down, anything to help relieve the pain in peace. I offered to help take some bags up to the room, as that would be my getaway for five minutes.

For the rest of the day the cramps came and went, although the sore throat was constant. I was hoping that maybe when I ate, it would get better. It's daft that even after being diagnosed with cancer I still believed I was indestructible and didn't recognise when something was seriously wrong.

Towards the end of the evening I was starting to waver

badly and knew I wouldn't last much longer, so I made my excuses and got a lift back to the house.

As I got ready for bed, I pulled the false eyelashes off as slowly as possible. When I had put them on I hadn't really thought about this part and I was terrified the whole lot would come out, but thankfully they didn't. I was so ill overnight that I spent the entire night getting up and down like a yo-yo. The cramps got so bad that I had to take the liquid morphine I had been given for the first time. I can't say if it worked or not, but judging by the fact that I made it through the following day in a lot less pain, I would imagine it did.

Monday 9th August

I had a friend coming over today with her new baby, who I would be meeting for the first time. The first part of the day my pain wasn't too bad and we went out for lunch, although I barely ate as the thought of food was making me feel sick. I thought everything was fine, but after she dropped me home things went from bad to worse. I was fighting so much pain that I contemplated calling the hospital, but I really thought I'd be wasting their time, as it was probably just a bug. However by 5 pm I was lying on my sofa in tears and that's when I acknowledged that something was seriously wrong. The pain was unbearable. I couldn't swallow. It felt as if there was a sharp block in my throat and the cramps were still going strong. I called the hospital, but could barely speak through my tears and pain. They told me to come straight in.

I couldn't do anything, unless I fancied getting a cab, which I didn't. So I decided to wait for Kate to get home. Luckily she pulled up within half an hour and between my tears I asked her to take me to hospital.

When we got there, I was given antibiotics pretty much immediately as a precaution. They also had to do a blood test, only this time I had made the mistake of sitting on the bed with nothing behind me, so when they tried to access the port the second the needle went in I flinched and the nurse had to pull away, leaving me a little bloodied and not looking forward to having to do it again. However, this time I moved to a chair, so I was prevented from falling backwards.

At some point they told me I was neutropenic, which didn't really mean a lot to me at the time. In fact my white blood cells had dropped. These are important for your immune system, so if I were to now catch a virus, I would be in trouble. They hooked me up to a saline drip again and I believe it was also administering antibiotics.

Overnight I kept waking with a really itchy neck, which very quickly turned into what looked like a rash. I can't say this was my most comfortable night, but pain always seems to ease off somewhat once you're in hospital and feel safe.

Tuesday 10th August

In the morning the nurses gave me some cream for my neck, which seemed to help with the soreness. Lucy and Kate came to see me, but they had to put on an apron and gloves before entering my room, which was a little comical.

Everything was going well until Dr Lowdell came in and dropped the bombshell - that I would be having a blood transfusion in the morning! I didn't even know I was still ill. As far as I was concerned I felt much better, so to say that this came as a shock would be an understatement. I believe that this time my red blood cells had dropped and that was what had led to the need for a transfusion. To be honest, it was all a bit beyond me and I didn't really know what was going on, so I figured I'd just have to play this one out and hope for the best.

Wednesday 11th August

I woke up in the morning feeling really nervous. It was the little things like this that tested me. I had never thought something like a blood transfusion would bother me so much, but for some reason, the thought of having someone else's blood running through my veins made me feel a bit queasy. I think the only thing that made me feel better was the knowledge that blood renews itself over a few months, so in theory what was about to be pumped into me would soon be replaced by my own new blood cells. I know it sounds stupid and I was more then grateful to all those who donate blood, it was just that I'd never really thought about it before.

When they brought the bag of blood in, I was transfixed. I was grateful that this would make me better, but still couldn't get my head around it. I watched as they hooked me up and as the first bit of blood ran through the tubes towards me. As it reached my arm, I could no longer look. I thought I'd feel something, but there was nothing; it was simple and pain free.

The whole process took about three hours, which is a long time when you're just sitting there. I was counting down the minutes, but unfortunately, just as it was about to come to an end, I was told I needed another transfusion. The light at the end of the tunnel, was that they told me that if my levels recovered I would be going home in the morning. With all that was going on today, I didn't know how I'd possibly be OK to go in the morning, but I was wrong. It's amazing how quickly your body can recover from some things.

Tuesday 24th August

I had my fifth session of chemotherapy today. This time it didn't go to my head like last time, so maybe I was getting used to it, although I wasn't looking forward to all the pills I'd have to take for the next three days. I was also slightly concerned, as I didn't want to end up back in hospital again like last time, so I figured I'd lock myself away for the rest of the week.

All went well and the week passed with not too much to report.

Wednesday 25th August

Today was the day I finally plucked up enough courage to shave all my hair off. Stupid worrying about it really, as there wasn't much left. Most of the sides and top was bald, but for some reason I still had a bit at the back and even with my headscarf on, this gave me a little bit of confidence, knowing there was still a little hair showing.

I made the decision that if I shaved it off it might help it to grow back evenly - time would tell with that one. I was also saying goodbye to my strawberry-blonde locks, as I was very aware that at my age they might grow back grey. I tried not to think about it too much and stayed positive.

Tuesday 7th September

I had to have my consultation with my oncologist a week before my chemotherapy this time, as he was going on holiday. It was a bit weird having to go in for a blood test and not get hooked up to anything.

During our conversation an oversight came to light - I was still taking the contraceptive pill, but I shouldn't have been. I didn't know this. As I was due to start taking Tamoxifen soon, I shouldn't combine the two, as the Tamoxifen wouldn't work properly if I did.

I was slightly miffed about this. I really didn't want to come off the pill, mainly because I used to get so ill and be in immense pain and the pill was the only thing that worked. It's an interesting fact though, which I wondered about all those years ago when I used to go through hell, that it was clearly all linked to hormones. So I wonder if my future was already mapped out. If the pain I experienced was an indication of things to come, was it all linked? I guess I'll never know.

Sunday 12th September

We were going to the Concert for Heroes in Twickenham, but I was really starting to struggle walking. I don't know where this new pain had come from, or even when it started. I was OK on the flat, but as soon as I started going up an incline the pain in my calves and the tops of my legs was unbearable and I had to keep stopping.

We took the short walk from our home to the local pub and I managed to grin and bear it, but only just, as it was becoming an issue. However, as usual, I figured it would pass.

When we got to Twickenham, we had what turned out to be a long walk to the stadium - at least it felt like forever to me. I was determined to make it and thought I could walk through the pain, but as it went on it was getting harder and harder. By the time we got to a bridge, I had to stop. I was starting to panic a bit as I thought I wouldn't make it and there were hundreds of people about, so I didn't know what to do except keep going. I found that if I stopped, the pain also stopped and I got a slight energy boost.

Finally we arrived at the stadium, but I was now faced with what seemed like a hundred stairs! I put my head down and took them one step at a time. I was so relieved when we got to our seats and wondered what was causing this new inability to lift my legs.

Tuesday 14th September

I was now on the home straight. My final chemotherapy session was today, and I couldn't wait for it to finish. During the session I noticed that my feet were slightly swollen, which was maybe why I was struggling with walking. When the lady did some reflexology (I was getting used to that) I mentioned it and she agreed, so we got the doctor to take a look.

She took me into a room, as she also wanted to check out my back pains. Nothing came to light and she was happy that the swelling was just water retention and not thrombosis or clots. However I was going on holiday in ten days, so I would still need to go back to check my blood counts.

My iron levels had also dropped. I didn't really understand this, but they recommended Spatone, which is an iron supplement and easily bought from a chemist, which would help bring my iron back up.

So now it was all over. It felt strange walking out knowing I'd never have to be hooked up again - at least I hoped so. Now all I needed to do was to return tomorrow for my injection, then again to do a blood test just before I went on holiday. Apparently I would also be keeping the port in for a few weeks, just in case there were any problems, which meant I still had one more general anaesthetic to go through.

CHAPTER SIX

Friday 24th September

Today Kez and I flew out to Cyprus for our week's holiday. My legs were really giving me grief and my feet looked more swollen then ever. I was slightly nervous about the flight, as I feared being in pain if they swelled further, and once we were in the air I wouldn't be able to do anything.

An hour and a half into the flight an attendant made a call for any doctor on the plane. Everyone started looking around, and it was evident that the focus was on a baby. She had been crying non-stop since we took off. A few minutes later the pilot announced that the plane was diverting to Münich, as we needed to make an emergency landing because of the child's illness.

When we landed, the plane hit the ground really hard and I noticed that we were followed down the runway by fire engines and an ambulance. It dawned on us later that the heavy landing would probably be due to the amount of fuel on the plane and that would be why the fire engines followed us. I guess if I ever experience that again I might be slightly worried!

The family left the plane and we had to await a slot to take off. A short while later we taxied down the runway, but then we came to an abrupt stop. The pilot told us that although he was ready to take off they had shut the airport because of a very bad thunderstorm!

This was the longest delay I've ever had on a plane - trust it to happen at a time when I really didn't need it. However, the pilot then announced that he would leave his door open and if anyone would like to ask him any questions they could go and talk to him. So, what's a girl gonna do but take the opportunity to check out the cockpit? It was something I'd always wanted to do. I was getting concerned though about being stuck on a plane and my legs swelling more, so I was trying to walk about as much as possible. Finally we were on our way and approximately seven hours after taking off we finally arrived in Cyprus.

This was the first time a stranger had approached me and asked if I was having chemotherapy, then told me his story. I think this is something I'd missed out on, as I'm such a self-contained person. I never spoke during treatment, so I never opened up to the support of those going through the same thing. It's daft really, and a lesson learned.

We got our transfer to our apartments and when we arrived, we had to walk through the complex to our apartment. This was when I first found out that I wasn't finding walking just difficult, but almost impossible. I had to keep stopping and could barely make it up a slight incline. I was praying that our apartment was not up any stairs. Thankfully my prayers were answered.

Once in the apartment I removed my shoes and socks and just stared at my feet. They looked as if they belonged to an elephant. I lay on the sofa and put them above my head, against the wall. I figured that by raising them they might get better. I found myself doing this every day of the holiday.

Saturday 25th September

It seemed like miles walking anywhere and I wasn't really coping. I couldn't bear the thought of stairs and even a few sent me into a panic. So we use the lift to get to the place where breakfast was served. By bizarre coincidence both of us had set our watches to the wrong time, so we were an hour behind and only just made breakfast before they started to pack up. Again, once breakfast was over, I opted for the lift to take us the one level up that we needed to go to get back to our apartment.

There were two pools at this complex, one pretty much outside our room and the other down a flight of stairs. The latter was clearly the nicer one and where everything seemed to be happening, but my energy was at an all-time low and for the first time ever on holiday, I didn't want to move or go anywhere. The stairs just filled me with dread. That's how bad my legs were - a short walk and I'd be physically drained. There was a family of three, who had also opted for this quieter pool and I would later discover we had something in common.

At lunchtime, we did finally make it back downstairs and took a short walk, or what felt like a shuffle in my case, down to the beach, which was basically a small rocky area where you had access to the sea. However the slope frightened me somewhat, so I only went down halfway before giving up. It's really strange - we often can't be bothered to do something, but this was real. I physically could not get down that slope and I was scared, as I couldn't understand it. Being in Cyprus wasn't helping as I knew I would never see a doctor.

Today was the day I discovered that sunbathing after your eyelashes have fallen out is something you have to be careful with. My eyes suddenly started to sting, and the stinging turned into pure agony. Nothing I did would take this sting away. My eyes were streaming for no apparent reason and I really started struggling in the pool, as if I wiped them the stinging got worse. It would be another 24 hours until I made the connection with the sun cream!

That night we got a taxi to the harbour front and for some reason, I suddenly felt fine. My legs now didn't seem to hurt, which was very welcome, so we made the most of it and did a bit of walking before dinner. By the time we got a taxi home I was flagging, but it was a good night painwise and I thought I was over the worse of it.

Sunday 26th September

I guess I spoke too soon. My walking had deteriorated. It's hard to explain because at first there is no pain; imagine trying to lift a boulder, but you physically can't do it. I physically could not lift one leg in front of the other, though I kept trying, and I think that's what made it worse. The only way I could continue was is if I kept stopping and standing still, which seemed to help me briefly regain some energy.

I had a feeling we wouldn't be doing much today, so I took my place by the pool for another day of hardcore sunbathing. While undergoing chemo you have to be careful in the sun as your skin is more sensitive, but a couple of weeks on I was making the most of it.

We started chatting to the family and discovered that the daughter was fighting a brain tumour and had undergone chemotherapy earlier in the year. I felt suddenly grateful for being able to talk to someone who had experienced this and ask them some questions I needed answers to.

My leg swelling in particular was my main cause of concern, but this lady had suffered the same, so I put this worry aside and figured it was normal.

The thing that struck me the most was that she was still struggling six months after chemo, and that frightened me a bit. You can't put everyone into the same category, as we are all individuals and our illnesses are all very different, but it didn't stop me fearing that I'd never get better.

Monday 27th September

Today we had decided to go to a local beach and thankfully we were offered a lift, so no walking was involved at the start of the day. I love going to the beach and this was no different. I was just a little sad that I felt so self-conscious and was worried my headscarf would come off, exposing my bald head to everyone.

I was really careful with the sun cream and kept it well away from my eyes, but once I was in the sun and in and out of the sea it somehow managed yet again to sting like crazy. The worst part was when we had swum out of our depth and I got salt water in my eyes. I might as well have swum back blind, as that's how it felt. However, the worse was yet to come, on our trek home.

We had been told which bus and the route it took back and the first part was fine. However when we got off the bus we had to navigate a dirt track, which in theory should only have been a ten-minute walk. It's really hard to explain what happened, but it felt a bit like slow motion. I took a slight stumble and put my leg out in front of me to stop me from falling, but there seemed to be no feeling in this leg. As it touched the ground, I felt nothing, almost as if my leg wasn't really there, and went crashing to the floor. Unfortunately this dirt track was very rocky and although I managed to put my hands out they ended up a little bloody.

I was now feeling real fear, and lay on the floor in silence for a few seconds. In those seconds my mind was working in overdrive. What if I really did have no feeling in my leg? What if I couldn't get up? I didn't understand what had just happened and it frightened me that I couldn't control my own body.

I had a deep cut in my finger and my hands were stinging like crazy. I knew I needed to wash them, sooner rather then later, as the last thing I needed was an infection. My immune system would still have been at its lowest and I didn't want to end up the same way as I had last month.

Slowly I got up and thankfully my leg did work, but I was nervous as I felt sure it would happen again. We took the rest of the walk slowly and I was willing the apartments to get nearer. When we finally arrived back, we cleaned my cuts and opted for a night in.

Tuesday 28th September

We decided to test out the big pool today, although getting there for me was still a mission. My eyes were getting worse and at lunch I could barely remove my sunglasses, as it just looked as if I was crying. This went on for about an hour. No matter how many clean tissues I used to dab them, they just continued to sting. I was starting to think that doing without sun cream on my face would be the only way.

In the evening we accepted a lift to the town for dinner. I was suffering badly. As we walked along the strip, I had to keep stopping as I had no energy to lift my feet off the ground. I was starting to get really worried now, as my legs resembled those of an elephant and the struggle and complete lack of energy I felt when attempting to walk was unbearable. I was extremely tired and not at all hungry. I had also noticed that my finger and toenails were going weird as they were forming holes at the bottom, which I kept picking at. These were to completely fall off within the next two weeks.

I felt I had put on so much weight that I didn't feel like me any more. Every night I had been sitting on the sofa with my legs up against the wall. Then I would sleep with them elevated on pillows, all in the attempt to drain the fluids. It didn't work. I swear my ankles were now twice the size they should have been.

Along with sitting by the pool, we also went back to the tiny beach, and this time I was determined to walk down the slope and into the sea. The worst thing was the actual process of getting into the water, as you had to walk on stones, sharp ones!

Thursday 30th September

Kez took part in the organised water aerobics. I would have liked to have joined in too, but it was evident that I would have struggled as my stomach was still not right. I couldn't even do a sit up, let alone jump around in the pool, and I was also worried they'd do stuff with your head under water, which for the same reason as yesterday, wasn't going to happen, so I just watched instead.

Friday 1st October

Day two of the water aerobics and I still didn't join in, but they did persuade me to play killer darts! I was so self-conscious that I didn't want to stand there, as everyone would see my ankles and my red eyes. In reality it would have been obvious I was ill and probably obvious that I had been having chemotherapy, but this didn't stop me feeling that everyone would stare. They didn't.

I had put on about 10 pounds during the chemotherapy, which I believed to be down to the steroids. During this trip I added another 10 pounds. I was the heaviest I had ever been, but didn't necessarily look it, as most if not all of it was in my legs. I was convinced that most of this weight was water retention and that this was restricting my movement.

Saturday 2nd October

When we arrived home in the UK at about 4 am I played down how bad I was really feeling. I already knew I would be going back to hospital. In theory I should have told Kez just to drive me straight there, but me being me, I went home, sorted my stuff out, said goodbye to her the next morning, then rang the hospital. Of course they told me to come straight in.

Kate wasn't home, so I was now in a situation where I either needed to get a taxi or attempt to drive. I stupidly chose the latter. The drive was horrendous and I should never have done it. My ankles were so swollen that I could barely lift my feet onto the pedals. I prayed I wouldn't hit traffic. Somehow I made it. It was weird though, every time I arrived at the hospital I instantly felt better.

They were worried about blood clots, which was something I hadn't considered. I had told them how I got breathless while walking, and this was something that could be linked to clots. I was terrified, I didn't really know what it would mean to have a blood clot, but I was pretty certain it wasn't good. So now I was in for another stint in hospital.

Sunday 3rd October

Today I had to have another scan, which I think was another CT scan. This time they really couldn't get the needle to do what it was supposed to. I wasn't really focused, but I believe they were trying to put a cannula in for the injection and it wouldn't go right. They said they would have to do the injection by hand, so instead I had to lie with a needle sticking out of my hand. To be honest I didn't really look, but it wasn't what you'd call comfortable.

After this I was taken to another room for an ultrasound scan on my legs before being taken back to my room. In the evening my oncologist came to see me and said it was all clear and more likely to be the steroids that were causing the swelling. However they would keep me in to monitor me.

Wednesday 6th October

Finally, this little episode came to an end. The swelling seemed to have reduced and I wasn't in so much pain any more.

Thankfully they discharged me, although I had a moment of panic when I remembered I'd have to drive home myself. I needn't have worried, as the drive home was much easier then the journey in.

It seemed weird to spend longer in hospital for swollen ankles than I had when I'd had an infection.

Thursday 14th October

Throughout all this I had constantly worried about work, so much so that they got me a laptop so I could keep up to date. I had also attempted to go in a few times, but I never lasted long and was always shattered by the time I got home. When the chemotherapy had started, I believed I'd have one bad week, followed by a slightly better one, followed by a week at work. It didn't quite work out like that and I had hardly spent any time at work since April. I had been due to go back on the 4th October, and since that hadn't happened I was now feeling a bit guilty. I just couldn't switch off from work. I don't know what's wrong with me, as I'd never fancied myself as a workaholic! But I feel guilty about not going back when I said I would, so today was the day.

Thankfully I had cover until the end of October, so I decided to go in, dressing in my jeans until then so that I didn't get drawn into anything. It was really hard, because apart from the hair loss I didn't look ill, yet if you took the chemotherapy out of the equation I had still had my stomach cut open hip to hip, and this hurt. My right arm had no feeling at the top and I still got electric shocks through my breast. I couldn't carry anything heavy, I was constantly tired and I was taking sleeping tablets on an almost nightly basis (although I still couldn't sleep). Combine all that with the after-effects of the chemo, which would probably last some time, and you'll understand why I was not really looking forward to the coming months. All this was also making me short tempered, so I wasn't too sure how my team at work would take to my return.

Thursday 21st October

I had an appointment with my oncologist today as I was due to start on Tamoxifen. I had read a few things about side effects and was slightly nervous. However someone pointed out that people generally only shout about bad experiences, so I should probably have stopped looking on the internet for answers. The prescription was free, thankfully, as you only get 60 days at a time and I would be on this now for the next five years.

The oncologist also warned me about the various side effects I might have, which could include hot flushes, swelling and nausea among others. For the first time I was panicking, as I thought that if I did get bad side effects, that would be what I had to look forward to for the next five years. He had told me I could take the medication at any time of the day, but before bed would be best, just in case I did have a bad reaction.

So that evening I sat wondering when I should take it. I made the decision that half an hour before a meal should be fine. I didn't like the idea of being kept awake by feeling ill, as I was having a bad enough time sleeping as it was. This turned out to be a big mistake. I had gone out to dinner with a friend and as my pizza arrived a wave of nausea overcame me and I could barely touch it. So I guess last thing at night would be better after all.

Thursday 28th October

My feet were a bit swollen again today. The swelling seemed to come and go, and today it was back. They looked a bit like tree trunks, but they were not nearly as bad as they had been.

Monday 8th November

Today was the day I finally had more surgery in the hope of giving me my body back. I had had no real problems that needed the use of the portacath, so it was coming out. But, more importantly, I was having a nipple reconstructed and liposuction to get rid of the overhanging fat on my hips.

At 12.30 Kate dropped me at the hospital. This - and I am touching wood as I write this - would be my final big hospital visit. I had all my details checked and they signed me in. I was taken to room 215 and within minutes a student nurse came in to take my details again and give me a wristband. She then took my pulse, temperature and oxygen. I was given a gown, stockings and again the paper see-through nappy pants.

Shortly after 1 pm, Paul Harris came to see me. We started

with photos; this was the first lot I had had since pre op in April. He then drew over me in marker pen, marking the areas where liposuction would take place, marked where the nipple would be and drew a ring around the portacath.

When he had left, the anaesthetist came in and checked my details - allergies, what time I went, nil by mouth etc. He then had a quick look at my veins and said that if there were any problems he would use the gas instead.

I was then wheeled down to the theatre. So many people ask you the same questions: 'What's your name? Date of birth? Did you sign this?'. I think at this point they were trying to distract me from the needle and anaesthetic going in.

I started to feel weird. The last thing I remember saying is 'I still find all this fascinating, even with this being my fourth time'. I was then out for the count.

I awoke slowly to hear the nurse say my name. It always takes a while to regain a sense of who you are and where you are. I went over my last words and thought I was still waiting to go to sleep. Then the nurse called me and I realised it was all over. I didn't feel any pain, but I did feel groggy. I just wanted to sleep.

I was taken back to my room and had to shuffle from the trolley onto my bed. That's when I felt the first twinge of pain in my hips. I also felt a stinging sensation where the port had been removed.

It was now 18.30. I had turned down offers of visitors, as I just wanted to lie in bed and sleep. I was attached to a saline drip and had to wait for that to finish before I could get into my pyjamas. I turned the TV off at 11 pm, then spent the entire night awake. My bladder had either shrunk or gone on some kind of overdrive, as every hour to an hour and a half I was up and desperate. It wasn't the pain that was keeping me up, as I still felt very little; it was my mind. I just couldn't shut it down, and for some reason all I could think about was bloody work!

At 3 am and 6 am a nurse came in to check my pulse, temperature and oxygen again. Just after 7 am a newspaper was dropped in and at 7.20 my surgeon came to see me to check everything was OK and arrange future appointments.

I now discovered why I felt no pain. I had had some local anaesthetic along with the general, which in theory should keep any discomfort at bay for 24 hours. So I guessed that the throbbing was yet to come. I also realised at this point that I no longer had any pain in my legs or ankles. I started tensing the muscles just to check, but no, there was definitely no pain. Maybe it was all the drugs I was on, but either way I was relieved.

Tessa picked me up at just after 11 am. I still felt fine and didn't feel like wasting a day resting, so off into town we went.

The bruises had already started to come out and my hips were very swollen.

Wednesday 10th November

I had a shower and dabbed myself dry where the dressings were and my white towel turned red. I looked down to try and establish where the blood was coming from and it was my breast; it seemed to be where the nipple was. It wouldn't stop bleeding and I started to panic, so I called a nurse. After convincing me it was nothing to worry about, she brought my appointment on Friday forward to tomorrow to have the dressings removed or changed. I spent the rest of the day with tissue shoved down my bra and added a bit more dressing. The pressure seemed to work and the bleeding stopped.

Thursday 11th November

I was offered last-minute tickets to a Harry Potter premiere. Not one to say no, I went off into London for lunch with friends, then headed to the hospital to sort my dressings out before returning to Leicester Square.

At 16.40 the nurse called me in, and I was nervous about what I was going to see. The bruises were still massive, so I was expecting worse under the dressings. She removed the ones on my hips first. I looked away quickly after getting a brief glimpse of what looked like a hole. I can only assume it was where the liposuction had taken place. Even now I still have a bit of a weak stomach.

She now started to remove the dressing from my breast. I looked down with a mixture of fascination and horror. My nipple looked abnormal, really big and just wrong. She explained to me that it would shrink to about 30% of the present size. I had faith in my plastic surgeon, as I believed he was the best, but even with that in mind I couldn't help feeling slightly nervous about this particular result. I guessed time would tell.

I went away with a bag full of tape, sponges and dressing. I would need to arrange to see a GP to remove the stitches in my hips in about 10 days - those around the port were dissolvable. I would be going back on the 6th December to see the surgeon to check on the nipple.

From Monday, I would need to change the dressing daily myself. This was not something I was looking forward to. I left relieved that all was well and headed to the premiere.

Friday 12th November

Today I was going to see *Phantom of the Opera*. I was very excited, as we had a backstage tour. It was a Christmas present from last year, but with all that had happened we had only just managed to confirm a date. My walking was temperamental - one minute it was fine and the next I struggled, which was making me a bit nervous about all the stairs backstage as I didn't want to hold anyone up. I figured that if we just kept to the back it would all be fine.

There was still a bit of bleeding, but it was now all covered with waterproof dressings and I was feeling more positive, as I was starting to see the end.

Saturday 13th November

My stomach was starting to look a lot better, though it was still slightly swollen and I had a hard lump on my back where some of the liposuction took place.

Monday 15th November

Today I decided to go back to work again. I was going to attempt to work short shifts, maybe 11.00 until 16.00, until I was 100 per cent. The thing I was most worried about was the journey to and from the office, as the drive seemed to wear me out. However, as predicted, this didn't go quite to plan and I was there until after 18.00 - just in time for the rush hour home!

I was also supposed to change the dressing on my breast today but for some reason I chickened out and left it. Anything medical still grossed me out, but I realised I would have to get it over and done with at some point.

Tuesday 16th November

I managed to pluck up the courage to change the dressing. The bleeding had stopped, but the nipple had done anything but shrink. I kept thinking, I know it'll be OK, but at this point, I just couldn't see how. I was looking at an abnormal-shaped nipple and imagining it would be like that forever. This was the only part I didn't include in my photo diary; I think I was too horrified to take a picture, which is a shame, because now looking back, it was quite fascinating.

Thursday 18th November

I made a slight error of judgement when I decided it was safe to remove the dressing on my hips, as the stitches were due out. However, as I pulled the tape off the left hand side the stitches seemed to be stuck to the tape and I pulled them off, along with some skin. It didn't look good and I panicked and pushed the dressing back on. I then did what I'm good at and got ready for work, trying to forget it ever happened.

Once at work, I called the doctor and booked an appointment for the following Thursday to remove the stitches. For some reason I failed to mention what had happened that morning. I was hoping it would be healed.

I worked from 10.30 until 18.30 again. I wasn't very good at easing myself slowly back to work. It looked as if I was going to have to give up trying!

Monday 22nd November

Today I had an appointment with my oncologist. My check-ups with him would start to become less frequent - the last time I saw him was six weeks ago. This particular visit does nothing for my nerves, as when he examined me he told me that the underside of my nipple was black. He told me to leave it a week and then give my plastic surgeon a call, as the tissue might have died. I took that as meaning the tissue *had* died, and therefore my nipple had been rejected and I'd have to do it all again.

I decided it would be OK at this point to be a drama queen. I also asked him when I'd get the all clear and be cured, as you always read about people beating cancer and the five-year marker and so on. This was crushed quite quickly when he explained that you never get the all clear. You are scanned and told you are clear of cancer now, which I was when I had my op and when I went back to hospital, but it can return at any time – it's just that after five years it becomes less likely. However the only real way to know if I'm *cured* is when I'm still sitting here in thirty years time. In short, there is no test that will give me or anyone else the news we really want to hear.

Tuesday 23rd November

I had a panic over my black nipple and despite being told to leave it a week, I called Mr Harris and managed to get an appointment for 14.30 that day at his Portland Street consultancy. Maybe I had panicked over nothing, as I was told it was fine and all I needed to do was to keep it clean until I went back to see him and get the final stitches removed on the 6th December. I think the blackness was just scabbing.

Friday 3rd December

For the first time in nearly a year, I drove to my parents' house. I hadn't been to Norfolk since my mum's funeral and was feeling anxious. We had organised a meal with the family for the next day and I was looking forward to seeing them.

I was on a subconscious 'This time last year…' countdown and was willing the hours to pass. It was strange that a year had passed, yet to me it still seemed like yesterday. I don't think

I had had the time to grieve properly, as my stupid illness got in the way.

Monday 6th December

I went to Parkside today to have the final stitches removed. I was still concerned that the underside of my nipple looked black, but it turned out to be fine. In fact most of the blackness was just dried blood, which he peeled off, although when doing so it looked as if part of my nipple had come away and it now had a big groove-like appearance, which in theory was an open wound in its side. I decided it could never possibly look normal again.

It's on days like today I am glad I have no feeling, though I imagine that would have really hurt.

Friday 10th December

I had been given a prescription for some special type of dressing, but when I went to the chemist they informed me it would cost over £70! So I opted for some much cheaper over-the-counter stuff. I also went back for a check up and all was fine. Thankfully my nipple had shrunk, just as they had told me it would.

Today was also the first day I went without my headscarf, three months after chemo had stopped. Roll on the next few months!

Today I went for what they call medical tattooing on my nipple. I had no idea what to expect, but it was the second time I was thankful of having no feeling in that area.

I arrived at the consultation suite in Portland Place (where the procedure would be carried out). Before they could start, I had to complete some forms which explained the procedure and give my consent. The lady carrying out the procedure explained to me that I would need two sessions and then a third within one to six years. However long the third one lasted would determine how often I went back in the future. This was because the tattoo would fade. I would imagine some women don't bother, so I guessed I'd have to wait and see if it bothered me.

She did suggest getting the other one done, to completely match the colour, but I am reluctant because I know I will very much feel it. We left it this time. On my next appointment I might decide to have it done.

She brought out a pack full of tiny jars of colour and matched one to me. I lay on the bed and turned away, numb or not, I still couldn't watch a needle! Needless to say, I didn't feel a thing except for a slight vibration. However it did bleed slightly, which made me more worried about doing the other side.

March 2nd

I couldn't believe it had been nearly five months since I last saw my oncologist, but today I had a check-up booked in. I thought it would be a simple chat and time for him to check me over, but no such luck. What I didn't know, although I found out very quickly, was that this check-up would involve a blood test, as they wanted to check my hormone levels. The initial appointment went fine; he checked me over and was happy with my progress. However then came the usual needle trauma, which was inevitable with the blood test!

Luckily for me, the nurse listened to me the first time and decided to get a doctor to do it, as she was well aware that my veins were almost invisible. At least half an hour and two attempts later, it was over.

My next appointment would be on the 20th April, for the colour touch-up with the medical tattooist. I wouldn't be seeing the oncologist for another six months, but I would be booking to see the breast specialist, who I hadn't seen since my operation, for a review shortly.

So here I was one year on. How did I feel at this point? I didn't really know. When you go through something like this, you start to re-evaluate your life. Suddenly, trivial things don't matter, or in my case they just annoyed me. But you do start to look at the bigger picture - where am I going, what am I doing, that sort of thing. Who knows where I'll be a year from now or what I'll be doing, I thought. But one thing's for sure, I need to make a change, one that will make my life less stressful and maybe seem rewarding. Until I figure that out, I'll just keep plodding on.

However, if I refer back to an earlier conversation with a nurse about Borneo and travelling, I was nearly there, as on the

3rd March 2011 I boarded a plane to Johannesburg to complete a two-week volunteer placement at the International Primate Rescue, in Pretoria. Not quite my orang-utans, but this was certainly something I would never have thought about doing a year before, and it was the most rewarding two weeks of my life.

So the final questions to ask were – would I ever get over it? Yes - it becomes part of your history, part of your story and soon to be a distant memory. Would I ever forget? No, and I fully expected to have moments of panic about the possibility of the cancer returning and could I go through it again? And finally, the lasting effects. I guess this is different for everyone, but for me, my eyebrows refused to grow back, so it was a constant reminder!

But the worst effect will always be the knowledge that I will never be a mum. That's the worse part of the disease for me, but that's now my own personal battle. So for now, I have decided to stop saving for a rainy day and instead life live exactly the way I want. I will do all I can to fulfill all my dreams from here on in.

This is a new chapter in my life, and this is also where I conclude this book, just a little over the twelve months since the start. I hope my story has helped show anyone who is struggling that there is light.

ND - #0447 - 270225 - C4 - 229/152/11 - PB - 9781909544376 - Matt Lamination